D1387737

THE
GREAT
CENTRAL
IN LNER DAYS

THE GREAT CENTRAL
IN LNER DAYS

David Jackson & Owen Russell

LONDON
IAN ALLAN LTD

First published 1983

ISBN 0 7110 1271 7

© Ian Allan Ltd 1983

Published by Ian Allan Ltd, Shepperton, Surrey;
and printed by Ian Allan Printing Ltd at their works
at Coombelands in Runnymede, England

Contents

1 (Frontispiece).
'Four-cylinder'. One of the most handsome of all GC classes
was the 'B7'. An impression of massive power is given in this
view of No 5481 standing at Woodford Loco in prewar
days. *G. Coltas*

Introduction

This book was written at the suggestion of the publishers, but the research on which it is based goes back to 1970. In the main this consists of the recollections of a large body of railwaymen that we have talked and corresponded with between then and the present. The task of setting out, filing and sifting this material has been in itself a considerable undertaking, quite apart from the writing of the book. Supplementing this basic core of information has come material from several different sources, including various official documents, notes and recollections of observers in different parts of the GC, photographs, and contemporary newspapers and magazines. We have done our best to leave no stone unturned.

It has been our impression that a very considerable proportion of railway literature deals first and foremost with the locomotive, covering its various mutations and transformations, and this feeling has led us to attempt a wider approach in the present work. We have tried to give a broad perspective of railway working, including features of operation and in many cases policy decisions. We have also endeavoured to present something of the general economic background and its influence on the railway.

Because of our good fortune in having access to records not previously available, it may be that some of the statements made in this volume will clash with previous accounts. If so, we can only stress that our views have always been arrived at in good faith, and that we have never at any time embarked on a particular project purely for the purpose of buttressing a specific point of view.

The task of attempting to thank all those who have helped in our researches is more daunting than the writing of the book. To single out the names of individual railwaymen who have given so unstintingly of their time, and

been such an inspiration to us in our projects, would swell this introduction to many pages. It must suffice to say that each one has contributed something of great value to the story, and that collectively it is the men at the 'grass roots' — drivers, guards, signalmen, yard staff, and other grades — who have made this volume possible.

Observers and students of the railway who have also assisted us include M. G. Boddy, H. D. Bowtell, W. A. Brown, W. Hennigan, K. Hoole, E. Neve, R. E. Rose, and W. B. Yeadon, most of them members of the RCTS 'Locomotives of the LNER' team. The research carried out by these individuals in their separate fields has in itself been a worthy example, and they have never failed to offer advice and suggestions when such have been sought. Mr R. H. N. Hardy, as railwayman and enthusiast, falls into both categories mentioned above; he was instrumental in launching us into our researches, and has never failed to help and encourage us ever since.

As far as possible the work of individual photographers is acknowledged with the illustrations, but we are pleased to take this opportunity of thanking them for the interest and enthusiasm they showed in our project; we also record our thanks to Mr B. Stephenson for so kindly placing the invaluable T. G. Hepburn photographs at our disposal. In all cases the response to our appeal was such that, inevitably, we were forced to make a number of very difficult decisions as to what to leave out.

And now we invite the reader to join us on the 'Birdcage', the raised walkway which linked the Beyer Peacock works with 'Gorton Tank' on the other side of the main line, so called because it was completely covered in with a wire mesh. It was traversed by generations of railwaymen and observers, and over the years has echoed with every type of GC chatter. It thus seems an appropriate vantage-point for a discussion of certain important aspects of the Great Central.

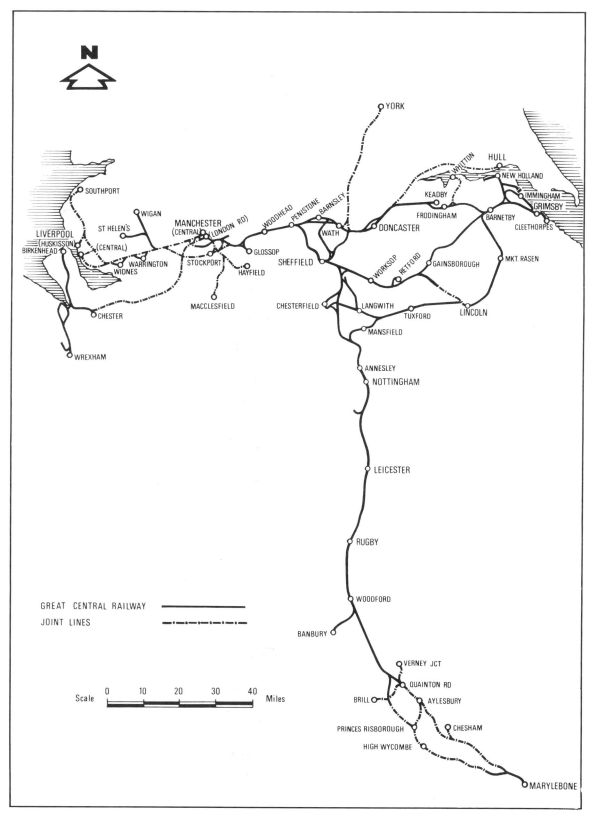

N

SOUTHPORT

WIGAN

ST HELEN'S

MANCHESTER
(CENTRAL) (LONDON RD)

WOODHEAD PENISTONE BARNSLEY

YORK

WHITTON HULL
NEW HOLLAND

KEADBY IMMINGHAM
FRODINGHAM GRIMSBY

LIVERPOOL
(HUSKISSON)
BIRKENHEAD

(CENTRAL)

WARRINGTON
WIDNES

STOCKPORT

GLOSSOP

HAYFIELD

WATH DONCASTER BARNETBY
CLEETHORPES

SHEFFIELD WORKSOP
RETFORD GAINSBOROUGH MKT. RASEN

CHESTER

MACCLESFIELD

CHESTERFIELD LANGWITH
TUXFORD LINCOLN

WREXHAM

MANSFIELD

ANNESLEY
NOTTINGHAM

LEICESTER

RUGBY

WOODFORD

BANBURY

VERNEY JCT

QUAINTON RD

BRILL AYLESBURY

CHESHAM

PRINCES RISBOROUGH

HIGH WYCOMBE

MARYLEBONE

GREAT CENTRAL RAILWAY ————

JOINT LINES —·—·—·—·—

Scale 0 10 20 30 40 Miles

7

Part One:
Thoughts from the Birdcage

1 Forward into the LNER

The companies absorbed into the LNER at the beginning of 1923 were all separate and distinct entities, each with its own customs, traditions and systems of working, and as the day of Grouping approached they must all have viewed each other with a certain mistrust, wondering what the future held in store. The characteristic of the Great Central Railway which distinguished it so sharply from its fellow constituents, apart from its position on the western edge of the new system, was the very aggressive and expansionist policy which it had followed ever since its progenitor the MSLR had astonished the rest of Britain by building a main line from Nottingham to London in the 1890s, thus placing itself among the elite group of companies owning a trunk line to the capital.

The new policy marked out the company as being in general considerably more progressive than those it was later to be teamed with in the LNER, except for the North Eastern Railway. The appointment of Alexander Henderson as GCR Chairman in the fateful year 1899 was to be the beginning of a change in the senior management which saw some of the most progressive people in the railway industry brought together to form a remarkable team. They included Sam Fay, General Manager from 1902, John G. Robinson who took over as Chief Mechanical Engineer from Harry Pollitt soon after Henderson became Chairman, Joseph Rostern, Superintendent of the Line, and A. F. Bound, the young and extremely forward-looking Signal Superintendent. The impact of these men was to be felt in a great many different ways in the years to come, and only a very few can be mentioned here. Once the enormous task of building up traffic on the new London line had got under way in the early years of the new century, other projects were quickly taken up. Extensive improvements were made to the very lucrative Yorkshire and Nottinghamshire coal traffic, including the building of a large marshalling yard at Wath which at that time was the most up-to-date in the country. Construction was begun on a brand-new deep-water port at Immingham, to be used for the export of coal and clearly intended to rival the NER and HBR installations on the other side of the Humber at Hull. Considerable portions of main line were doubled and resignalled, and at the other end of the system a completely new line into London was built in concert with the Great Western, serving the important towns of High Wycombe and Princes Risborough.

The programme of improvements flowed on into the years of World War 1, including the building of the Doncaster Avoiding Line and the provision of the new lifting bridge at Keadby, and the GCR also had a sub-

stantial share in the promotion of yet another new line, the Mansfield Railway. The fact that Immingham was in the hands of the Admiralty during the war served to promote a busy coal traffic, and the port may be said to have received its baptism of fire in more senses than one during these years.

Under the LNER, Henderson, now Lord Faringdon, continued to be the guardian of GC interests as a result of being appointed Deputy Chairman of the new company, a position he continued to hold until his death in 1934. His influence is to be discerned principally in the goods and mineral field, as by 1923 it had become apparent that the GCR passenger services had reached a peak of development beyond which only limited future growth could be anticipated; the latter had in any case earned little if any real revenue, and the real money-spinners had always been the mineral services. Thus we find that one of the first suggested schemes to affect the GC under its new owners was a proposal for the electrification of the Woodhead route, which was chiefly important for the enormous tonnages of coal conveyed between the Yorkshire and Nottinghamshire pits and the industrial regions of Lancashire. This appears to have been originally put forward about 1926, but was not in fact to be put into practical effect until some years later.

Another proposal directly affecting the GC interest was the programme of improvements at Frodingham, in connection with the expanding iron and steel industry in that part of the world. This involved a complete reconstruction of the railway facilities, including provision of new yards, new passenger and goods stations, and a modern locomotive shed. Extending over several years from about 1927, the complete series of works constituted the largest civil engineering project undertaken by the LNER.

Lord Faringdon's interest in the fish trade, another important aspect of GC traffic, was to be seen in the plan for a new fish dock at Grimsby which was first discussed about 1930; the Deputy Chairman actually cut the first sod when work commenced not long afterwards, but he had died by the time the project was completed. Another posthumous project which may be traced to his influence was Mottram Yard, opened in 1935 to serve the Woodhead coal traffic, but planned during the last vigorous years of his life. It can be seen from these examples that the former GCR leader exercised a considerable sway among his colleagues on the LNER board, and these improvements hint at a vigorous continuance of the policies which had brought his former company into the forefront of railway affairs.

Alas, Faringdon's greatest enemy, and the enemy of all

the country's industrialists, was the depressed state of British trade. To a greater extent than almost any other railway company, the GCR had built its traffic round the traditional industries which had been the means of Britain's rise as a great manufacturing nation during the 19th century, in particular coal, iron and steel, and to a lesser extent cotton. It is probably true to say that the coal traffic was the essential life-blood of the GCR, developing originally along the Woodhead route and expanding in other directions after the turn of the century; the whole purpose of the Immingham project, and allied features such as the building of the Doncaster Avoiding Line, take-over of the LDECR and the share in the Mansfield Railway, was to facilitate the movement of coal. Sadly, the severe decline in what was to become after 1920 a depressed and strike-ridden industry was to affect GC traffics drastically.

Much the same may be said of the iron, steel and heavy engineering industries. Apart from the relative prosperity of sections of the Frodingham district and Shotton the picture of general depression was almost completely unrelieved, although as far as the GC system was concerned it escaped the severity more usually associated with these sectors in the North East and the West of Scotland. Nevertheless, many large and famous firms were shut down for extended periods. Penistone was declared a national disaster area when the steelworks in the town closed for good and elsewhere the important steelmaking centres of Sheffield, Rotherham, Stocksbridge, Irlam and Brymbo were all affected by depressed markets. The great engineering cities of Sheffield and Manchester were also badly hit by the decline in trade, especially during the early 1930s. Beyer Peacock's Gorton Foundry, for example was on a care and maintenance basis by 1933. The fortunes of all these concerns, in a very real sense, was mirrored on the GC network. Revival came through the demand for steel in the automotive trade and re-armament.

A small indication of the basic soundness of the GCR schemes may however be seen in the fact that, despite the generally black picture, exports of coal via Immingham increased considerably between the wars, and also the London line was to see a steady increase in mineral traffic, nearly all of it going on to the GWR via the Woodford-Banbury link. Had the prevailing climate of trade been at all favourable, there is little doubt that these traffics would have handsomely repaid the parent company's investments. Mineral traffic on the London route was to reach a stage of development where special high-speed trains were introduced, known as 'Windcutters', plying between Annesley and Woodford, which was the busiest section of the route.

The perishable traffic handled by the GC covered a wide range of foodstuffs, including fish, meat, dairy products, vegetables and fruit. Of these, the first-named was probably the most important, based of course on Grimsby. Complete fish trains left daily for London, the north-west, and the Midlands, and it was customary for many passenger trains to depart from Grimsby Town station with odd fish vans attached at the rear. The traffic

expanded considerably between the wars, with a rise of 10,000 tons of fish in the total of fish landed for 1928, as against 1922, and the opening of a new dock has already been referred to. However the GC services did not feel the full benefit of this development because from 1924 the London traffic was diverted to run via the East Lincolnshire line of the GN Section, which was more direct and a good deal less congested than the original GC route. Under this arrangement the working of the London fish was transferred from the GC men to the former GN shed at New England.

Meat and dairy products were transported from Liverpool and Immingham to inland destinations, and the main artery for vegetable and fruit traffic was the Lincoln-Manchester line, along which passed vegetables grown in Lincolnshire and the Fen country, fruit from East Anglia, and commodities imported through the London docks.

The GCR operated a busy general goods service, running services in conjunction with the NER, GNR and GER, as well as its own through trains between Manchester and Marylebone. At the time the London line was built it was anticipated that the goods traffic would expand considerably, but the expectations were not fulfilled; this was due not so much to the decline in trade after World War 1, as to the phenomenal growth of road transport, the other great enemy of the railways during the interwar years. In the conveyance of smaller loads, which the general goods traffic consisted of in considerable part, the road hauliers were frequently able to offer a service that was both cheaper and more efficient. In all probability however, it was the GN and GE Sections which suffered the most from this form of competition, as the large volume of vegetable and fruit traffic associated with the eastern half of England was also a prime target for the road operators. The LNER speeded up its goods services during a comprehensive retiming of all principal trains early in the 1930s, but it seems doubtful whether this manoeuvre had much effect in preventing the loss of certain very lucrative traffics to the road hauliers.

Apart from an early and notably unsuccessful experiment with a Pullman train, operating initially between Kings Cross and Sheffield, and later running to Manchester, together with a few alterations in the spring of 1929 which are discussed in Chapter 7, the GC passenger service remained remarkably little changed in these years. As already suggested, the point of maximum development had probably been reached with most services; the north-south trains were competitive only on the section south of Sheffield, and apart from the exception discussed in Chapter 7, remained unaltered beyond slight adjustments to the running times. Much the same was true of the cross-country service operating between Liverpool and Hull, and the Continental trains linking Liverpool and Harwich, although both these services were comparatively well-patronised.

Custom on the Manchester-London services increased from about 1934, when trains began to load up to 9 or 10 vehicles, or even more on occasion, but this was partly due to new regulations permitting the use of excursion tickets on normal trains. The general rise in excursion traffic was a more encouraging feature of the period, particularly in the 1930s when many people were better able to afford regular holidays and days out in the summer. A considerable increase in special traffic connected with Association Football was also apparent, and the GC was particularly well placed in this respect with its direct access to Wembley Stadium, and also proximity to such venues as the Sheffield Wednesday ground at Hillsborough, and Manchester United's headquarters at Old Trafford, both the latter being frequently used for FA Cup semi-finals and occasionally even internationals; during the 1930s a special station was opened to serve the Manchester United stadium on match days. Another important ground was that of Huddersfield Town at Leeds Road, accessible from the GC via the LYR from Penistone; the Huddersfield club's tremendous successes between the wars attracted huge crowds, and the ground was also in demand for Cup semi-finals.

At the opposite end of the social spectrum, the GC also did good business in promoting the well-known and always well-patronised cruises from Immingham. The 'Orient Line Specials' operating from Marylebone and Manchester became a regular GC feature during the summer.

Also in the 'special' category were the Marylebone-Newcastle overnight trains which began to operate in the spring of 1937, mainly as a means of relieving the congestion at King's Cross. These of course survived into the postwar era as the 'Starlight Specials'.

W. G. P. Maclure had been Locomotive Running Superintendent of the GCR ever since the post was first created at the end of the 19th century, and under the LNER he was appointed Loco Running Superintendent of the Southern Area, that part of the new company embracing the territories of the former Great Central, Great Northern, and Great Eastern Railways. His is a career which has so far received little attention in railway literature, yet as head of what was in effect a completely separate department in GC days, and entirely so after 1923, he had a bigger part to play in the sphere of locomotive deployment and utilisation than either J. G. Robinson or Nigel Gresley, the two Chief Mechanical Engineers with whom he worked.

Beginning as an apprentice at Gorton, he later had spells at Staveley and Grimsby and worked for some time as a travelling inspector before eventually being appointed Running Superintendent. In this capacity he was nominally responsible to the Chief Mechanical Engineer, but seems from the first to have enjoyed considerable autonomy. He was in charge of equipping and staffing the locomotive running sheds, and took a special interest in improving the standard of footplate work by encouraging the formation of Mutual Improvement Classes and supporting the Locomotivemen's Craft Guild. He was also mindful of the men's welfare, encouraging them to join trade unions at a time when such bodies were usually detested by members of the management, and also promoted ambulance work. His popularity amongst the employees, not surprisingly, was legend.

Evidence of Maclure's dominion over the LNER Southern Area is to be seen in the utilisation of GC engines in locations outside the GC, particularly on the GN Section, and also in the retention of native engines on the best GC passenger work, despite the presence of more modern types such as Classes A1 and D49, both of which were tried on the Manchester-Marylebone line. In the latter case there is no doubt that he was influenced by the feelings of the footplatemen, who were very prejudiced against the products of Doncaster. In all probability the policies followed by Maclure underlie many other happenings which took place in the Southern Area, and his career deserves further study.

His decision to transfer various GC engines to other parts of the LNER is a reminder of the fact that in general the stud of Gorton-designed locomotives which the new company inherited in 1923 were of recent construction, and the proportion of very old engines correspondingly smaller. In addition there were a number of types which, though built in the early years of the century, were able to give reliable service throughout LNER days and in many cases far beyond, thanks to their solid and durable construction; these included Classes J11, Q4, N5, C13 and C14. Another feature of the Gorton method of locomotive building was the extensive use which was made of standard parts; several classes of engine were constructed almost entirely of parts usable in other types, and thus the practice facilitated the development of new types as well as cheapening construction. It also permitted simplification of storekeeping.

In wagon construction the GCR showed itself to be well in touch with the latest developments. Bogie fish vans were introduced in 1903 and bogie coal wagons in the following year. The latter were of an extremely modern design, being metal-bodied and, most unusually for mineral vehicles at that early period, vacuum-fitted; 30-ton and 40-ton variants were put into service, their use permitting significant economies to be made in the working of traffic. Unfortunately however they could not be very widely used because of the special facilities required for handling vehicles of such size, and they were mainly confined to the task of transporting loco coal to the sheds on the London line. The notion of conveying coal in high-capacity wagons marshalled in fast vacuum-fitted trains was of course highly typical of Great Central thinking, but because of the limitations mentioned it could not be put into practical effect, and the wagons were withdrawn from service during LNER days.

Sets of new passenger coaches were built at the Dukinfield Works shortly before Grouping, coming well up to the modern standards apparent in so much GC equipment. Put to use on the principal expresses, they incorporated John G. Robinson's patent anti-collision buffers, which had been tried out on earlier units during the war; they were designed to prevent the telescoping which according to a number of accident reports was a major source of danger to passengers, and their adoption affords evidence of the concern for safety which animated the GCR management. They are known to have been involved in accidents at Marylebone and Grimsby, and were commended in both. The stock fitted with the buffers was displaced on the principal services in the late 1920s by LNER coaches of Gresley design, and incorporating the patent buckeye couplings which it was claimed acted with the same effect as the Robinson apparatus.

Thanks to the advanced ideas of A. F. Bound, Great Central signalling was in the front rank by 1923. His innovations included pneumatic signalling, installed on the main line between Manchester London Road and Newton, colour-light signals in the vicinity of Marylebone, and above all the advance warning system patented under the name of Reliostop. The first experimental installation of this apparatus was made in 1916 between Marylebone and Wembley Hill on the GW&GC Joint Line, and three years later the system was extended, being taken out as far as Harrow South Junction. A single example was also positioned at Crowden on the western approach to Woodhead tunnel, a location chosen for the purpose of testing the equipment in more extreme weather conditions. Most of the Class 9N passenger tanks, all of which were based in London, were fitted with the corresponding locomotive attachment, and later engines were built new with it immediately before Grouping. No official information has been traced about this apparatus, and it is not possible to say how far it was regarded as successful; it had a short life under the new ownership, and the reasons for its removal are not known. It seems safe to say however that the LNER was antipathetic to safety devices of this kind, since at a later date the Raven fog-signalling apparatus was removed from the NE Area, this being in much wider use than Reliostop.

Because of its late entry into the field of trunk-line working, the Great Central had to make much use of advertising, and over the years its posters became justly famous as it strove to bring the virtues of its services to public notice. The LNER continued in a very similar vein, producing some of the most attractive advertising material to be seen anywhere in Britain, and it is not without significance that from the mid-1920s the post of Advertising Manager was held by C. G. G. Dandridge, a former GC man. The practice of naming locomotives, obviously allied to advertising, was another important part of the GC inheritance, and we can be sure that when the policy of naming engines was seriously taken up by the LNER from 1925, the Deputy-Chairman was fully in support of the idea.

Nepotism is not an uncommon feature of business concerns, but few can have taken it further than did the GCR. The board was probably unique in including the son of the Chairman, Eric Butler-Henderson, and it is even more remarkable that despite having joined the GC board only four years before Grouping he followed his distinguished father on to the LNER board, a single family thus representing 50% of the GC interest. Another interesting example was W. G. P. Maclure, who was the son of Sir John Maclure, a director of MSLR days. John G. Robinson's son Matthew became District Loco Superintendent at Neasden, and E. W. Rostern eventually became Superintendent of the LNER Southern Area after his father Joseph had been the last GCR Chief Goods Manager. Sir Sam Fay's eldest son, S. E. Fay, acquired the position of Assistant Traffic Manager of the GCR Southern Division, but left the company in 1920. Perhaps the feeling of belonging to a 'family firm' made these curiosities seem less remarkable to the staff. The presence of so many scions of formerly prominent figures in the old company may have helped to preserve a more noticeable GC atmosphere and to give a sense of continuity, and it perhaps helps to explain why so many of the staff remained somewhat 'Great Central minded' even many years after Grouping.

2

2
The Chairman: No 6169 *Lord Faringdon* pauses at the up end of Penistone station while on a typical Gorton No 2 Link turn of the 1930s. The driver is believed to be David Bailey. *Real Photographs*

3
The hub of the GC. The smoky atmosphere of Sheffield Victoria did not attract photographers, but here is a nice study of Gorton's 'B7' No 5035 on an up express in 1930. *G. Coltas*

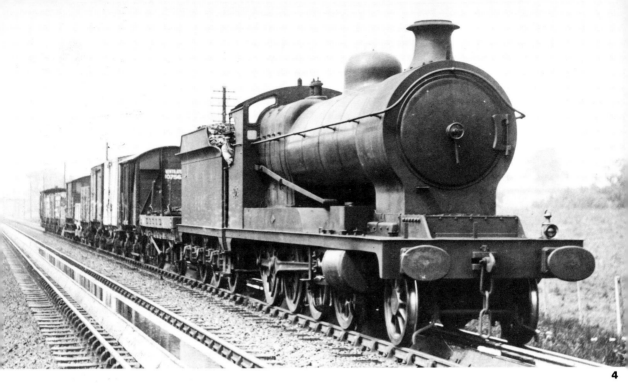

4
'O4' No 6282 of Annesley is at Charwelton up troughs
en route for Woodford about 1930. *Real Photographs*

5
Northbound coal empties were a characteristic feature of the
Annesley-Woodford section of the GC. Langwith's 'O4'
No 6537 approaches Charwelton, just north of Woodford,
on 3 July 1937. *L. Hanson*

2 The Inverted Image of the Great Central

The image of the Great Central which has been projected through most railway literature, especially the material published between the wars, conveys in some respects a false impression of the company. To attempt to adjust this, in however small and incomplete a way, is one of the aims of this book.

The difference between the GCR and other companies was that it was, in a sense, two systems in one. The London line was still a very new phenomenon even at the time of Grouping, and because of the outbreak of war in 1914 the company had not been able to develop its traffic to the full; or perhaps its traffic could not be developed beyond a certain point because of the over-competitive situation which existed between the various trunk lines. Some aspects of this matter have been discussed in the previous chapter. Whatever the reasons for it, the line south of Nottingham was somewhat sparsely occupied, and presented a contrast to the rest of the system, where on many lines there was intensive activity and even congestion. An observer accustomed to the near-chaos of Woodhead working would, if he chanced to visit the section of line south of Woodford, have had some difficulty in believing that he was still on the same system. The truth is that, throughout the period covered by this book, the 'London Branch' as it was sometimes nicknamed, was of limited consequence compared with the busy routes in the vicinity of Manchester, Sheffield, Doncaster and north Lincolnshire. The building of the London line and the subsequent immense efforts to prosper its services are events of great historical importance, all faithfully reflected for instance in Mr G. Dow's *Great Central*, but in the full tale of purely commercial achievement they are not, alas, of great moment.

The contrast between the two parts of the GC has received little attention in railway literature, and what was actually happened is that the London line has received considerably the more coverage of the two, in such material as has been published. In the days before World War 2 when comparatively few railway books appeared, the student of railways gleaned a good deal of his knowledge from periodicals, and especially the *Railway Magazine*. At the time such material was highly topical and up-to-date; today it forms an invaluable reservoir of historical matter upon which retrospective accounts can be based. For whatever reason however, the articles, photographs and other material dealing with the GC usually tended to be orientated towards the southern end of the system. This may perhaps have been because the contributors were people who lived in the south, or because the editors felt that material dealing with the southern end of the system would be more appreciated by the readership. It is not the purpose of this book to criticise the editorial policy of the *Railway Magazine*, for it never failed to maintain a high standard of excellence, and the authors have invariably read it with interest and

enjoyment; there can be little doubt however that most of the GC material published in the period under review obliges the reader to look at that system through the wrong end of a pair of binoculars.

We find places on the London Extension mentioned with some frequency, yet such venues as Manchester, Sheffield, Mexborough, Frodingham or Immingham appear decidedly rarely. It is of course true to some extent that this leaning towards the London end of the trunk routes may be found in material relating to other companies. Even today, when one considers the large amount of published matter dealing with the Great Northern main line, one is conscious of a strong southerly flavour. Much is made of Kings Cross and the lines in its immediate vicinity, but we hear comparatively little of such places as Doncaster, the importance of which certainly exceeded that of anywhere else on the GN system.

Omissions of this kind may be more or less grievous according to one's personal interest in a particular area, but in the case of the GC it would not be going too far to say that the head and heart of the system has been almost entirely left out of the reckoning. In the sphere of locomotives and their working, for example, the student of GC affairs will quickly realise that no shed on the system could approach the importance of Gorton. Yet one searches in vain for published sources dealing with this important centre.

An interesting insight may be obtained from an analysis of the 'British Locomotive Practice and Performance' series of articles published every month in the *Railway Magazine* throughout the period with which this book deals. These articles were accompanied by logs set out in tabular form, and in the period 1923-39 there were a total of 103 such logs relating to the GC Section. Of these, 11 were recorded on the Manchester-Sheffield portion of the route, 25 between Sheffield and Nottingham or on some part of this, and 67 between Leicester and Marylebone; the reader will hardly need to be reminded that the last-named was the most southerly part of the route. The majority of engines logged were from Leicester Loco, with several of the articles being devoted entirely to the work of that shed insofar as they concern the GC Section. Few logs appeared dealing with work done by Gorton engines, and the shed itself is seldom mentioned in the series. Where a Gorton turn is included in the logs there is no mention of the engine's origin, and in some instances one has the impression that the author, the late C. J. Allen, was not actually aware that a Gorton engine was being timed. Going through the series of articles in sequence, the reader gradually realises that the author was considerably more familiar with the Leicester-Marylebone part of the GC than with its northern end. This is shown not only in the larger number of logs relating to the south, but also in such details as drivers' names; a considerable number of Leicester men are mentioned by name, and a few from Neasden, but not one solitary Gorton man appears to have gained this distinction.

Clearly, the emphasis apparent in Mr Allen's articles is somewhat unfortunate from the point of view of a balanced version of events. Here again we do not wish to appear to criticise the author; he was after all not concerned with presenting a history of the GC, balanced or otherwise, and simply chose to publish those items which best fitted his purpose of discussing engine performance and train-timing. But there is no doubt that his choice of material was characteristic of the general trend already mentioned.

There were a number of trials and other important locomotive developments at Gorton of which very little, if anything at all, reached the readers of railway publications. Chapter 10 tells how the LNER Garratt was tested on the Woodhead line in the spring of 1925; the importance of this occasion was recognised by the local press, and there were both reports and photographs of what took place. By any standards the trials of this Garratt, the first of its kind to be built for a British railway company, was an event of some importance, and it is difficult to believe that nothing was ever written about it in the *Railway Magazine* or some other railway publications. Yet such appears to have been the case. It was only as a result of quite fortuitous circumstances that a few meagre details of this came to light recently.

As an instance of something equally important in a slightly different way, the spring of 1933 saw the first use of new Class B17 engines on the long through working between Manchester and Marylebone. This was the first time non-GC engines had been regularly employed on these important turns, and it marked in many ways the beginning of a new era, as is described in Chapter 4. Contemporary issues of the *Railway Magazine* carry a few photographs of the trains concerned, but the importance of what was happening does not appear to have been grasped, and nothing of it is conveyed to the reader. Yet we note an odd contrast with the treatment accorded to the later 'B17s', the 'Footballer' series, when the first batch of these were sent to Leicester Loco in the spring of 1936; they received a great deal of attention in the 'British Locomotive Practice and Performance' articles, and were spoken of as though the type had been newly introduced to the GC. Yet they were really no different from the earlier series. It hardly needs to be added that the latter were stationed at Gorton.

A very interesting locomotive trial took place at Gorton early in 1927 when the first of the new Class D49 'Shire' engines, No 234 *Yorkshire*, was put to work for a short spell on GC Section expresses. It appears to have worked no further south than Leicester, but so far as the authors have been able to discover these were the first turns performed by a passenger engine of pure LNER design in the Southern Area, and were thus of some significance; yet little if any mention of these things reached the printed page. However when another of the class, No 245 *Lincolnshire*, worked for a spell from Kings Cross Loco in 1928-9, by which time the engines were no longer new, the occurrence attracted attention in the

Railway Magazine, presumably because some rather better-known trains were involved. Such omissions, we feel, are more likely to have been the product of chance rather than of deliberate editorial policy, but there is no doubt that they have helped to contribute towards the topsy-turvy picture of the GC which is the subject of this chapter.

A further aspect of the north-south contrast concerns the difficulty of the road. It is well-known that the Manchester-Marylebone line was one of considerable severity from a gradient point of view, but of course the notorious climb to Woodhead was by far the worst stretch. Whether approached from east or west it ranked as one of the hardest climbs on any British main line, and besides the gradients it contained curvature severe enough to restrict downhill speeds to a considerable extent — this of course being a favourite device to regain time lost during a climb. It was also subject to extremes of weather not so frequently encountered south of Sheffield. Probably the most severe test set to a GC express passenger engine in the normal course of working was the climb from Sheffield to Dunford Bridge following a through run from Marylebone, the exertion being in no way diminished by the stop at Penistone as the train then had to be restarted on the steepest part of the whole gradient, marked at 1 in 100. In his book *Great Central Steam*, the late Dr W. A. Tuplin describes as 'pitiable' the efforts of a 'Green Arrow' engine to restart a train of eight coaches at this notorious location. The ascent to Woodhead undoubtedly called for the very best in both locomotives and men, and if the task was added to, as it often was, by the conditions of a typical Pennine winter, then we begin to reach some understanding of what the GC Section engines and men had to contend with. So far as we are aware, no runs of this kind were included among those published in the 'British Locomotive Practice and Performance' series, but clearly such work constituted the true measure of 'performance' as far as GC Section engines are concerned. Had more information of the very detailed and accurate kind published by C. J. Allen been available in respect of the Woodhead section, we might perhaps have gained a deeper understanding of the capabilities of both GCR and LNER engine types used on express passenger work.

It is possible also that some light could have been thrown on at least one rather confusing discovery. As a result of research carried out amongst railwaymen it has become clear that at Gorton the Class B17 engines were very unpopular; the point is amply confirmed in what seems to be the only previously published account of Gorton before 1939, namely S. C. Townroe's *The Great Central As I Knew It*. The fact that the Gorton men disliked the 'B17s' so much forms a curious contrast to the glowing reports of the 'Footballer' engines in C. J. Allen's articles, or O. S. Nock's verdict after his run with No 2841 *Gayton Hall* on the 2.32am from Marylebone. If more information had been available about how the 'B17s' fared at the northern end of the route, then perhaps this matter could have been resolved. It seems likely that the gradients of Woodhead had a good deal to do with the attitude of the Gorton men, and in this context some accurate logs would have been of very great value.

In the realm of published photographs it is possible to detect the same leaning towards the London end of the system. Of the numerous photographers whose work appeared in such periodicals as the *Railway Magazine* up to 1939, only two or three chose to submit pictures showing the northern end of the GC; the two most important were Dr P. Ransome-Wallis and the late R. D. Pollard, although it is clear that only a small part of their output actually appeared. It is unfortunate that so few of the photographs taken by the late W. H. Whitworth should have been published, as he captured many very typical views of the GC Section in the Manchester area. Sheffield, sometimes described as the hub of the GC, seems to have suffered particularly badly; very few pictures of Sheffield Victoria were ever published between the wars, and the spot does not seem to have attracted photographers, perhaps because of the bad atmospheric conditions which frequently prevailed there. Places such as Mexborough and Frodingham were very rarely photographed, it seems, probably because they were off the main express passenger routes and so were more closely associated with the unspectacular mineral engines; yet their importance in the GC system can hardly be exaggerated, particularly that of Frodingham, which was extensively developed under the LNER. Photographs were taken in the vicinity of Grimsby by F. H. Gillford and T. E. Rounthwaite, but the results have not been published.

By contrast, the 1923-39 issues of the *Railway Magazine* contain many lineside views taken south of Leicester, and other photographs were taken at Marylebone and Neasden Loco; the last-named was quite a popular spot as it was very well placed for photography, especially in the evenings.

In more recent years the work of a great many lesser-known photographers has come to light, and apart from the exceptions mentioned above it is now clear that the GC Section was in fact very well served in this respect; it is to be hoped that in time more of this material will be published. There were, for example, a number of photographers active in Nottingham between the wars, their work offering a very wide coverage of GC operations in the city; prominent among them was the late T. G. Hepburn, some examples of whose work are included in this book. He has left behind a collection of material which deserves to be recognised as an outstanding monument to the memory of the GC.

The most recently published album of GC photographs, *Great Central Recalled*, is in some respects an interesting echo of the *Railway Magazine*. Out of a total of 74 photographs whose location is readily recognisable, it contains 36 taken at Leicester or further south; there are none at Sheffield, and only a very few taken in Lincolnshire. This is not to suggest of course that the album is in any way spoilt because of these features, but such an emphasis does have the effect of presenting places such as Leicester as being more important than Manchester or Sheffield, though obviously this is not intentional.

In most railway literature there is a clear division between passenger and goods activity, and it is usually the former which claims the greater share of attention; the reasons for this are too obvious to need explanation. In the case of the GC, there can be no doubt that the passenger services offer a fine example of the enterprise and efficiency which were an essential part of the company's outlook, but in terms of revenue their importance was negligible. Throughout its history the Great Central was basically a mineral and goods line, its most important work being the haulage of coal, iron, steel and fish in that order. In this respect it contrasted sharply with the other companies which were brought together in the LNER, and especially its two partners in the Southern Area, the Great Northern and Great Eastern. Therefore the pre-occupation with passenger services tended, in however small a way, to work to the disadvantage of the Great Central, if only because its fast passenger services were comparatively sparse.

For the authors to pretend that the present volume will avoid the pitfalls mentioned in this chapter would be presumptuous. To prepare a comprehensive account of the Great Central at any particular period of its existence, reflecting faithfully the relative importance of its various traffics, would require a book very much larger than this one, and would entail research on a scale far exceeding anything the authors have attempted. Nor would we wish to suggest that any of the literary or photographic matter referred to is in any sense lacking in merit because of the points mentioned; all this material, ultimately, is grist to the writer's mill. Our aim is nothing more than to make the reader aware of certain aspects of the Great Central which, in our opinion, will help to give a true insight into the real nature of the company. We cannot however pretend that even this limited aim has necessarily been achieved, and ultimately the reader must be the judge.

6
Penistone station, up end, in GCR days. The works at right was the Cammell Laird establishment, closed in 1930 and subsequently demolished. *Biltcliffe & Co*

7
'C4' No 5266 of Leicester on an up express at Dunford in 1927. The down sidings at right were on a falling gradient, specially constructed to assist westbound trains into Woodhead Tunnel. *Real Photographs*

3 Gorton

If there has been some neglect of the northern end of the GC system, as has been suggested, then the most serious result of this is that no proper assessment of the position occupied by Gorton has so far appeared. In making this small attempt to remedy the deficiency, the authors can do no more than touch the fringe of this very considerable subject; the story of Gorton is in many ways the story of the Great Central itself.

Though it could not be described as the heart of the GC in a geographical sense, Gorton was its heart in virtually every other respect. The imposing premises situated on the GC main line a couple of miles east of Manchester London Road incorporated the locomotive building and repairing works (always known as 'Gorton Tank' by local people, despite the fact that the whole complex was actually in Openshaw), carriage works, and the largest and by far the most important running shed on the system. All this was crammed into a teeming site located in the heart of one of Manchester's more dingy inner suburbs, and the reader will not be surprised to learn that lack of space was a major problem for the management. This applied especially to the loco running shed.

In earlier MSLR days the shed had no doubt been adequate for its purpose, but the steady development of services which culminated in the opening of the London line brought much additional work, and the allocation of engines rose in proportion. From the last years of the 19th century onwards the man chiefly responsible for this process was the Locomotive Running Superintendent, W. G. P. Maclure. Under his jurisdiction came the crucial task of planning the allocation and diagramming of all the company's engines, and as his office was at Gorton it was perhaps not surprising that some of the best work on the system should be operated by Gorton men and engines. He was on the closest of terms with the local footplatemen, among whom he appears to have been universally loved and respected. Because of his benevolent despotism Gorton main line men were unrivalled in their road knowledge, and worked a variety of both passenger and goods turns which would have put the roster board of any other shed well in the shade.

However the increase in work inevitably produced congestion. The requirement for a larger number of engines, and their steadily growing size, together with a huge increase in the volume of rolling stock, created problems of movement which could only have been fully solved by enlarging the site. Alas however, the GCR complex was hemmed in on every side by an agglomeration of housing and industrial premises which left not a square inch of space for extension. The best alternative was to hive off part of the capacity and accept the inconvenience of resiting it further from Manchester; this is the story behind the building of the new carriage works at Dukinfield in 1907.

Even this was not a complete answer however, and by Grouping the movement of engines at Gorton Loco was still a round-the-clock problem for the Running Foremen.

The situation is well described by George Free White, one-time Gorton District Locomotive Superintendent, in an article published in the *LNER Magazine* of December 1927:

'All engines passing to and from the shed have to pass a very congested point owing to the fact that at the outlet of the running shed yard everything going to and from the erecting shops, locomotive paint shops and the Gorton works yard has to pass this point... The result is that nearly every movement has to be controlled by fixed signals, and the movement of an engine from one road to another frequently has to depend upon the working of traffic between the various points mentioned; consequently, unavoidable delays often take place in getting engines from the coal stage into the various roads where they have to be finally berthed.'

Though these words were written over four years after the LNER came into existence, they are just as true of Gorton at Grouping. By then there were approximately 200 engines on the shed's allocation, in premises which were originally designed to accommodate less than half that number. Manpower employed in the Loco Running Superintendent's department included over 300 sets of footplatemen, a small army of cleaners working in gangs under their foremen, and numerous auxiliary workers whose tasks varied from office work to shed labouring. To most observers Gorton Loco appeared overworked and overstaffed; it was the scene of non-stop activity night and day as engines came and went, crews and other workmen swarmed here and there as they went about their tasks, all to the constant accompaniment of locomotive whistles, and at times almost blotted out by a pall of smoke as engine and factory chimneys belched forth their contents.

The location of Gorton was most easily identified by the long frontage of the erecting shop on the up side of the main line. It ran parallel with the latter and was separated from it by a fence behind which could usually be seen such items as spare boilers, tenders, cabs and other impedimenta associated with locomotive building and repairing. The roads giving access to the Loco diverged from the main line near the Manchester end of the erecting shop building and curved away behind it, the shed itself being at right angles to the line and virtually out of sight of it. The roads leading into the erecting shops formed a junction with the Loco roads near the point of divergence from the main line, and on these could usually be seen engines waiting to go in for repair, standing nose to tail without tenders. With very rare exceptions, all engines of GC origin were repaired at Gorton during LNER days, apart from ex-ROD Class O4s allocated to the NE and Scottish Areas. In later years certain LNER-type engines were also sent to Gorton for repair, as will be described presently.

Hidden from the main line as described, the Loco was also out of sight from the surrounding streets because of its high walls, and for those without an entry permit the only view was from the 'Birdcage', a feature which Part One of this volume affectionately commemorates in its title. This gave access to Wellington Street (later renamed Widnes Street), a cul-de-sac running at right angles to the main line and on which was an entrance for enginemen and shed employees.

Parallel with Wellington Street across on the opposite side of the shed was the original carriage works, a distinctive building forming a background to many photographs. Described in a Manchester street map of the 1920s as 'Carriage Repairing Shop', it contained equipment for carrying out running repairs, and also housed sets of main line coaching stock for two of the most important GC expresses, the 2.15pm up and the 3.20pm down London trains. The latter was generally regarded as the showpiece of the GC Section, and it was characteristic that its coaches should be based at Gorton. For several years following Grouping the stock was of the latest GC pattern, built at Dukinfield shortly after World War 1, and these continued in use until the introduction of sets of new Gresley stock in 1929, after trials with an initial set about 1927. Between the wars the cleaning timetable remained the same; the empty carriages arrived from Manchester Central shortly after 8.15pm, and were then taken in hand by the cleaners and examiners on the nightshift. By the time the vehicles reappeared next day to form the 8.20 up express, which was the companion outward working, they were said to shine like a mirror inside and out. Running repairs were carried out as necessary during the night.

Sandwiched between the carriage shops and the Loco was a smaller establishment, the Locomotive Paint Shop, accessible by means of roads running parallel with the main Loco roads. Here newly overhauled engines were brought by one of the Works pilots to receive the final treatment which, in the case of large passenger engines especially, excited so much admiration amongst observers. When leaving the paint shop the engines were handily placed for the Loco, where they were taken in hand by the Trial Trip crew to have their first test run.

The main Loco building dated from 1879 and was of the old-fashioned 'blind back' type, the very worst layout from an operating point of view. It incorporated 20 roads, each finishing up at a set of buffer stops against the wall. Immediately in front of the building was a row of pits, one on each road, and it was here that ash disposal was carried out.

The two most prominent structures on the Loco yard were the pulverising plant and the coal stage, both at the far right as one faced the shed frontage. The former was a kind of tall metal tower erected in late GCR days for experiments with pulverised fuel; it fell out of use when the experiments were discontinued soon after Grouping and was dismantled about 1928. The coaling stage was a raised and roofed platform approached by long ramps; it was served by two roads, one for the 'best' coal used by passenger and fast goods engines, and the other for ordinary coal. All coaling was done manually with aid of the GC-type steel tubs.

To have the coaling stage so close to the shed building was a disadvantage because of the need to bring loco coal wagons into the shed yard, and the congestion was further added to by the presence of wagons used for ash disposal; G. F. White has recorded that 250 tons of ash were removed from Gorton Loco every week. The need to eliminate these wagon movements from the shed yard had long been realised, but it was to be nearly 10 years after Grouping before a scheme of improvements was put in hand, embodying a complete resiting of the coaling and ash disposal services. A new installation consisting of one of the latest 'Cenotaph' type coal hoppers, only the second of its kind to be erected on the LNER, and modern ash disposal facilities, was positioned well outside the loco yard, on a group of roads at the side of the main line. From then onwards the view of operations from passing trains was much improved, as on most days two or three rows of engines were always visible on these adjacent roads, waiting for coal or disposing of ash. With the demolition of the old coal stage the shed yard became much more roomy, and the elimination of so many wagon movements effected a great simplification of working. This made possible the dismantling of the yard signals, and the signalbox which stood adjacent to the curve leading to the shed was disconnected and used as a store, being popularly known as the 'Lighthouse'. These improvements brought about great economies in time and labour.

Other buildings which deserve mention in connection with the Loco, though a good distance away from it, are the sponge cloth laundry and the dormitory used by visiting enginemen and guards. Both were on the perimeter of the complex, accessible from Cornwall Street, a thoroughfare running parallel with Wellington Street and to the east of it. The dormitory, always known as the 'barracks' in common with other similar buildings on the GC Section, had originally been built by the MSLR as a school for employees' children; it made a suitable barracks because its distance from the Loco ensured a measure of quietness for the occupants. The sponge cloth laundry was situated between Cornwall Street and the waterway running parallel with it, which was the Stockport branch of the Manchester & Ashton-under-Lyne Canal. The use of sponge cloths in preference of cotton waste for engine-cleaning purposes had resulted in considerable saving of money; dirty cloths were received at the laundry from sheds all over the Southern Area, and after first having had the oil squeezed out of them they were washed and returned for further use. The dirty oil was used for lubricating points.

The Gorton complex lay at the heart of a district devoted almost entirely to heavy engineering of one kind or another. Near neighbours included one of the most famous of all private locomotive builders, Messrs Beyer Peacock & Co, whose premises directly faced the works on the opposite side of the main line; their products were regularly sent all over the world, and newly-built engines were frequently to be seen standing in a siding adjacent to

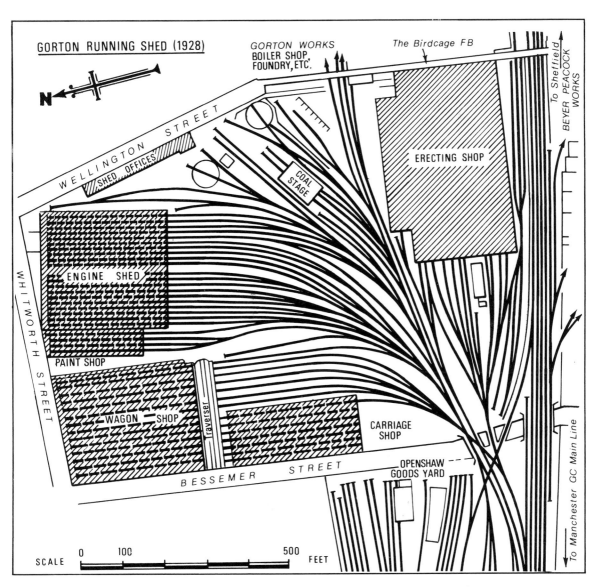

GORTON RUNNING SHED (1928)

N

GORTON WORKS
BOILER SHOP,
FOUNDRY, ETC.

The Birdcage FB

To Sheffield

BEYER PEACOCK WORKS

WELLINGTON STREET

SHED OFFICES

WHITWORTH STREET

ENGINE SHED

COAL STAGE

ERECTING SHOP

PAINT SHOP

Traverser

WAGON SHOP

CARRIAGE SHOP

BESSEMER STREET

OPENSHAW GOODS YARD

To Manchester GC Main Line

SCALE 0 100 500 FEET

Fig 1
A plan of Gorton Loco originally published in the *LNER Magazine*.

the main line, awaiting delivery. The links between Peacock's and the GCR had alway been very close, and the connection was to continue into LNER days; apart from building a number of engines for the new company, the firm also tested their products occasionally on the GC main line; the well-known but unsuccessful Beyer-Ljungstrom engine for instance made its first trials on the GC.

Alongside the Carriage Works was the Openshaw Works of another industrial giant, Sir W. G. Armstrong Whitworth & Co; they were involved in various kinds of heavy engineering and had produced naval ordnance during World War 1. A little way beyond this building

and adjacent to Ashburys station was one of the two Crossley factories in the vicinity, the other being alongside Peacock's. These two works operated as separate concerns, the latter producing the well-known Crossley buses, lorries and cars. This factory overlooked Belle Vue Loco, formerly of the Midland Railway, a modest establishment reached by means of a junction on the main line immediately east of Ashburys station. Other engineering concerns in the vicinity included the Vaughan Crane Company, Messrs Brooks and Doxey, and in later years Messrs Ferguson Pailin, manufacturers of electrical equipment. There were a great many smaller firms dotted about, all specialising in one branch of engineering or another, and the district formed a huge concentrated pool of engineering skill and experience which was second to none in the country. During LNER days 'Gorton Tech' was built on land adjacent to Ashburys station, and here generations of students and apprentices mastered the theoretical side of their craft; the establishment could claim to produce men trained in a whole range of engineering skills.

The industries of Gorton suffered varying degrees of depression as the economic climate worsened between the wars. 'Gorton Tank' itself was no exception, being considerably affected by LNER reorganisation even before the really hard times began. Following the new company's decision to concentrate the building of new engines at Doncaster and Darlington, the works was never again to see the sort of activity that had been the norm in GCR days. In the period up to 1939 only a handful of engines were built there, the most notable probably being the two Class S1 humping engines constructed to J. G. Robinson's original design of 1907. To utilise the spare capacity the LNER diverted a considerable amount of repair and other auxiliary work to Gorton; for several years after Grouping the works was responsible for preparing ROD engines for service after their purchase from the Government, these of course being of original GCR design; the works also assisted in running-in new engines built elsewhere, including examples of Classes A1, K3 and D11, the last-named another original GCR design of course. In later years Class J39 and B17 engines were scheduled to come to Gorton for periodic overhaul, the appearances of the latter being much appreciated by local observers. Valuable though they were, these measures failed to keep the works occupied to full capacity; the number of staff was reduced, and during the slump years it became the practice to dismiss apprentices when they reached the end of their time.

The promotion of W. G. P. Maclure to the position of Loco Running Superintendent of the LNER Southern Area in the 1923, and his consequent transfer to a new office in the former GER buildings at Liverpool Street, did not in any way weaken his close ties with Gorton Loco; he visited it regularly at weekends, and exerted the same kind of benevolent authority as in GCR days. As a result the work done by Gorton men and engines remained as interesting and various as in the past, and was probably unique on the whole of the LNER.

A complete range of duties was covered, from the best express passenger turns on the GC Section down to the humble pilots which shunted the Loco and Works Yards. In between came fast and medium goods workings to all parts of the LNER except the north-east and Scotland, a huge amount of local passenger work associated with Manchester London Road station, and a substantial share in the almost endless procession of mineral trains from Yorkshire and Nottinghamshire.

The links responsible for carrying out all this work were arranged in order of prestige on the roster board, beginning with the illustrious No 1 Express Passenger Link, or Top Link as it was usually known. The crews comprising it were in charge of the most important passenger turns, which in the main were through passenger workings to Marylebone, and later on the Continental turn which was worked as far as Ipswich; all of these were lodging jobs. Next in order of precedence came the No 2 Express Passenger Link, which was the exact opposite of the Top Link in that none of the turns involved lodging; most of the work was on fast passenger trains between Manchester and Sheffield, and consequently this was a very popular link because of the fairly regular hours, and also the very small amount of night work.

Closely rivalling the two fast passenger links in prestige was the No 1 Fast Goods Link, or 'Pipe Train Link' as it was called because of the fully-fitted trains which were worked. These went principally to London and Lincoln, the 7.50pm to Marylebone Goods being the original 'Pipe Train'; the turns involved a not particularly pleasant combination of lodging and night work, but in spite of this there was never any shortage of recruits because the Pipe Train Link was the essential stepping-stone to the senior passenger work, and when vacancies occurred in the express passenger links they were normally filled by fast goods men. To keep their hand in on passenger trains the latter had first option on the working of weekend specials, as and when their normal duties allowed.

All the drivers in the Fast Passenger and Goods Links were on the closest of terms with W. G. P. Maclure, and their continuance in these important roles was due entirely to his blessing; among this elite body dismissal from the footplate was unknown, and demotion exceptionally rare, at least up to the time of Maclure's retirement.

There was a profusion of other goods workings to a variety of places, including Hull, Grimsby, Lincoln, Nottingham, Leicester, Whitemoor and Ardsley, and initially most of this work was the preserve of individual crews who were often the only ones possessing the necessary road knowledge. From about 1930 onwards they were reorganised on a conventional link basis.

Local passenger work was the concern of the 'Tanky Links', as they were called for obvious reasons. The redoubtable 'tanky' engines, mainly Parker 2-4-2s, worked trains to Macclesfield, Hayfield and Hadfield, sharing the work with engines and men from the sub-sheds at the far end of these lines. Some of the drivers spent many years on this work, which was popular for the usual reasons — no night work, and reasonably regular hours by railway standards. Furthermore many of the men were reluctant to move on because they disliked the added responsibility of express work, and lacked the confidence to tackle it; they were happy to settle for a career of shuttling up and down the same familiar stretch of line until the day of retirement, or as happened in some cases, until deteriorating eyesight enforced a change.

The endless string of coal trains for which the Woodhead line was famous provided work for a very large number of Gorton crews, the links being divided into those employed on lodging work and those on out-and-home turns; an example of the latter was the 'Barnsley Junction Turn-Back Link', where the drivers worked what in effect were glorified trips with coal empties and loads. Lodging jobs took the men to places such as Annesley, Retford, Langwith, Mexborough and Barnsley.

Nearer the bottom end of the scale were the Pilot

Links, who were in charge of shunting in the various yards east of London Road. The most important were Guide Bridge, Dewsnap, Ardwick and Ducie Street, while other locations included Dukinfield Carriage Works, Fallowfield, and Gorton Works and Loco. These links were usually composed of younger crews, with the firemen often getting their first taste of regular footplate work, but there were also a number of elderly drivers who had come off main line work because of poor eyesight, injury, or indifferent health; because of this the Pilot Links were sometimes referred to as the 'Old Men's Links'.

There was a variety of relief links which covered everything from berthing engines on the shed to relieving crews of main line expresses at Guide Bridge, Gorton & Openshaw or Hyde Road. Of these the so-called 'Cover Link' claimed distinction as it consisted of men with extensive road knowledge capable of deputising for main line drivers at short notice; all Cover Link men were hand-picked, and were earmarked for greater things in time to come. The presence of what were in effect future Top Link or fast goods drivers created some unusual nicknames, including the 'Shining Light Link' and the 'Green Mustard Link'.

The large amount of lodging work will have been noted, and this was very much a feature of life on the GC Section. If a man hoped to rise to the top of his profession he had to be prepared to go almost anywhere and to spend a great deal of time away from home; footplate work on the GC was not an ideal occupation from the point of view of home and family life. On companies such as the GNR and NER there had been a great falling-off in the amount of lodging work following World War 1 as a result of union pressure, and the men had come to regard it as a practice properly belonging to the Edwardian era. No such changes took place on the GC, and the mode was well typified at Gorton, where at any time of day or night one might see a procession of men commuting between the Loco and the barracks, and where Yorkshire and Lincolnshire accents mingled with the distinctive Mancunian twang, with occasional Cockney or East Anglian interpolations.

Lodging work was not of course unpopular with everybody. The extra money always attracted those who took a pride in their bank balance, and the work was also a means of escape for men not on the best of terms with their spouses; some drivers worked lodging turns for years without a break. The men's wives almost invariably disliked lodging, because apart from their husband's long absences there was the chore of preparing a very substantial food basket, with three or even four meals requiring to be packed.

Promotion at Gorton was to some extent a matter of chance, particularly where the best work was concerned. The number of men aspiring to this was obviously much greater than the places available, and most drivers got no further than the coal train links. The fast passenger and goods drivers were men who had at some stage rendered a signal service to the Company, whether it was a readiness to volunteer for some particularly unattractive task, or to work during a strike; such things were taken careful note of by W. G. P. Maclure. Firemen gained experience on the top work by attaching themselves to a particular driver as opportunity offered, perhaps on a weekend special working for example, and making the best possible impression. Favouritism and nepotism were clearly an integral part of the system, although never to the extent of impairing efficiency; if a train ran late because of bad firing, the man responsible would wait a long time before having another chance to prove himself. In the period between the wars, as earlier, the driver's authority was absolute, and he could make or break a young fireman merely by a nod or shake of the head. All drivers were treated with a mixture of fear and respect by the younger staff, and those on the London lodging jobs were looked upon, to coin Lord Beaverbrook's phrase, as 'Men like Gods'.

A system of seniority was inaugurated by the unions shortly after Grouping, the main principle being promotion according to length of service. This was ignored at Gorton for some years, and then from about 1931 it began to operate with regard to firemen only.

The Gorton Top Link at about the time of Grouping included Willoughby Lee, Benny Goulden, Enoch Bell, Bill Chapman, Billy Davy and Tom Davies, all of whom had started on the MSLR in the 1870s and 1880s. By 1931 they had all retired and a new generation was in charge, among whom were Jimmy Rickards, David Horne, Algy Roberts, Jim Rangeley, George Bourne and Jack Glover. Long-serving members of the No 2 Link included Bob Barlow, David Bailey, Jim Fielding, Fred Cross, Ernie Fretwell, and Arthur Minshaw. Cover Link men who later aspired to higher things were Bill Flanders, A. G. Warren, Jack Hopley, Bill Yeomans and A. E. Dakin. Drivers particularly associated with fast goods work were such as Jerry Riley, Tom Seaborne, Harry Wynne, Jack Winstanley and Charlie Neave.

Another figure of importance was the Trial Trip driver, who was in charge of testing newly-overhauled engines by taking them on a short trip, usually to Hadfield, and then examining them and booking defects. The occupant of this post at Grouping was Jack Howard, later the first regular driver of the 'Continental'; he was succeeded by Joe Chamberlain, one of the small number of ex-Dinting men to achieve distinction at Gorton, and after Chamberlain's death came Ernie Calvert. All the Trial Trip drivers were experienced main line men.

In earlier LNER days it was almost invariably the case that when a new class of engine took the rails, one of the first representatives found its way to Gorton. In 1924 a whole series of new Pacifics were sent there for running-in, and were used on a variety of turns including a few through trips to London. Scottish 'Directors' and new Class N7 0-6-2 tanks were also seen at about the same time, mainly on local services, and in 1925 a batch of new 'K3s' was tried on the fast goods workings. In 1927 the first 'Shire', No 234 *Yorkshire*, worked in the No 2 Link for a short time. Poppet-valve 'B12s' built by Beyer Peacock's were to be seen in 1927-8 and were also used in the No 2 Link. 'B17' No 2802 *Walsingham* was sent to Gorton in December 1928, being the very first of its class to go into regular service.

This phase of activity has given rise from time to time to speculation about plans for a programme of locomotive standardisation, but it is more probable that these events testify to the influence of Maclure, who was always ready to see that his confreres at Gorton had an opportunity to sample whatever happened to be available. Had the men expressed a wish to make use of a particular type, the appropriate arrangements would have been put in hand. To talk of 'standardisation programmes' on the GC therefore is to ignore completely the influence of Maclure, and the unusual relationship he had with Gorton. It was only after he retired that any trend towards standardisation became apparent, and even this was very gradual. It is also noticeable that after his retirement the visits of new locomotive types to Gorton came to an end.

We take our leave of Gorton by glancing briefly at a typical shed scene as it appeared at a particularly interesting time, the date being 30 March 1935. This was shortly before a major invasion of LNER types began, an event which was presently to alter the traditional Gorton image very considerably. For many years it was customary for members of the Manchester Loco Society to visit Gorton on Saturday mornings and to be conducted round the shed in a party; many typical scenes have thus been placed on record through the enthusiasm of this devoted body.

Altogether 62 engines were noted, all save 10 being of GC origin. As already mentioned, this was a proportion which was soon to alter. Providing a vivid splash of green amongst the predominating black were three of the very handsome 'B17' engines, two of which, Nos 2811 *Raynham Hall* of Stratford and No 2819 *Welbeck Abbey* of Cambridge, were being run-in after overhaul in the adjacent works; both had gone in in January, and No 2811 had been out a fortnight when it was noted, and No 2819 a week. The third 'B17', No 2825 *Raby Castle*, was from Ipswich and had arrived in Manchester the previous afternoon with the down 'North Country Continental'; it was now awaiting its return working on the corresponding up train. At this period Gorton had only three 'B17s' on its strength, none of which were visible at the time of the visit; No 2816 *Fallodon* had gone to Ipswich the previous day on the up 'Continental', No 2840 *Somerleyton Hall* was in London awaiting return on the 3.20pm down, and No 2841 *Gayton Hall* was under repair in the works.

There was a variety of GC express passenger types on view, prominent amongst them Neasden's No 5437 *Prince George*, which had reached Manchester the previous evening with the 3.20pm from Marylebone, and now stood prepared to work home with the 2.20pm up train. Gorton's No 6169 *Lord Faringdon* was present, this engine having now suffered something of a decline in prestige as it was restricted to the humbler No 2 Link duties along with certain Class B2 and D10 engines; it was probably being prepared to work the 12.40pm Manchester-Cleethorpes express, for which it would be due off the shed at 12.15.

Two rather unusual visitors were on view in the shape of 'B1' No 5196 of Woodford and No 5258 *Viscount Cross*, stationed at Immingham; the latter had just been repaired and was booked back to traffic on the day it was noted. During the next few days it would be put on a few running-in turns before being sent back to Lincolnshire. The 4-6-0 cannot be accounted for quite so easily, as Woodford engines did not work to Manchester on normal diagrams and only rarely on specials; this engine had been repaired and put back to traffic on 2 February, and may have been kept at Gorton if giving trouble.

Two 'D9s', Nos 5112 and 6019, completed the tally of express passenger types. The former, a Retford engine, had been booked out of the works a week previously and was noted as having been newly painted. No 6019 was a Sheffield engine, and may have come to Gorton after working an early-morning turn to Manchester London Road.

Local passenger types were represented by a group of the faithful 'F1s', Nos 5589/98/99 and 5731, together with 'F2' No 5777 and 'C13s' Nos 5115 and 5357. All these were stationed at Gorton except the last-named, which belonged to Trafford Park and is believed to have worked in on an empty stock turn from Manchester Central to the carriage sidings at Ardwick.

The Class B7 fast goods engines formed an interesting group, for in addition to Gorton's No 5470, one of the short-chimney series, there were two Neasden engines, Nos 5460 and 5461, and also No 5467 of Immingham. One of the Neasden engines would be rostered to work home on the evening 'Pipe Train' from Ardwick East. The Immingham engine had just been repaired and was booked back to traffic on the day seen.

The Class J11 'Pom-poms' were represented by eight examples, Nos 5123, 5202/11/42/81/90, 5302 and 6011, these 0-6-0 general purpose engines always being well to the fore at Gorton. All were locally based except No 5281, from Lincolnshire, and No 6011 of Annesley.

Seven 'J39s' were on view, representing by far the largest non-GC contingent on that occasion. Three of them were Gorton engines, Nos 1255/98 and 1497, while 1273 and 1493 were from Lincoln, 1277 was from Retford, and 2781 from Annesley. The two Lincoln engines would work home on mixed goods trains, one of them being normally booked for the 12.58pm Ardwick-Lincoln goods. The visitor from Retford would have arrived in the early hours with an overnight goods from Retford Low Yard, and would begin the first stage of its return journey on the 3.52pm stopping passenger train to Sheffield.

The remaining engines were 'N5' 0-6-2 tanks for pilot duties, a solitary 'J62' 0-6-0 tank, No 5883, and of course a large collection of 'O4s', mostly Gorton-based, but also including visitors from the usual 'coal' sheds — Nos 6244 from Sheffield, 6266 from Annesley, 6308 from Colwick, 6569 from Frodingham, 6574 from Immingham and 6634 from Langwith. The heavy mineral section was completed by two Retford engines, 'Q4' No 5065 and 'O5' No 5419.

Last on the list was 'L1' No 5275 the familiar 'Crab' which was allocated continuously to Gorton for over 25 years, and unique as the only example of its class to be based in Manchester during LNER days. It worked invariably at Guide Bridge, being in charge of the heaviest pilot work.

Apart obviously from the LNER types, the engines mentioned in this list might well have been seen together at Gorton at any time from 1923 onwards, and so the scene may be taken as typical of the shed during its most important days. The list therefore not only gives an indication of the work being done at a particular period, but also serves as a memorial of this most important of Great Central sheds.

8
This view of No 5430 *Purdon Viccars* at Gorton Loco on 30 July 1933, while it was being run-in after repairs, gives some indication of the dazzling finish which was applied in the paint shop. *G. Coltas*

9
Gorton Barracks is the only part of the original complex still standing at the time of writing. This view of 1 March 1982 shows the distinctive frontage, still as it was in LNER days. *Mrs G. Taylor*

10
Unusual visitor: 'B12' No 8520 is on Gorton turntable on Sunday 30 July 1933 after an unaccustomed working. The enginemen's entrance off Wellington Street is directly to the rear of the tender. *G. Coltas*

11
Gorton in April 1936, from the top of the coaling hopper, looking east. In the foreground are the new servicing facilities installed by the LNER — ashpits and loco coal wagon sidings. The access to the shed from the main line can be seen near Priory Junction signalbox, at right. The 'Lighthouse' signalbox is still intact though out of use by this time. Behind it is the erecting shop and to the right of this building the 'Birdcage'. The actual locomotive shed is out of sight at the left, but was at right angles to the main line. *W. Potter*

12

13

14

12
'N5' No 5918, pictured at Gorton Loco on the same date, is typical of the 0-6-2Ts used widely on the GC Section. At far right may be seen the remains of the coal stage, in process of demolition. *G. Coltas*

13
Gorton Loco Yard in May 1935. 'O4' No 6326 is a visitor from Langwith, while the 'F1', 'F2' and 'N5' tanks are locals. *W. Potter*

14
Coaling, old style. The original Gorton hand coaling-stage was a building which had a certain character. The engines are 'J10' No 5820 of Gorton, 'J39' No 1287 from Leicester, and an unidentified GN 0-6-0. The 'J39' was probably at Gorton after working the overnight Leicester-Manchester goods. *W. Potter*

15
Immaculate 'D10' No 438C *Worsley-Taylor* on Gorton Loco soon after Grouping, probably ex-works. This photo is on the same spot as that of 'N5' No 5918 (photo 12) and the coal stage may be seen in the background. *Real Photographs*

16
Coaling, new style. The 'Cenotaph' mechanical coaling plant photographed in May 1935. Brought into use about 1933, Gorton's plant was only the second built on the LNER, the first being at Doncaster. *W. Potter*

16

17
Running Repairs. Not all repairs to locomotives involved visits to Gorton Works. Here is No 5104 *Queen Alexandra* under the sheerlegs at Leicester Loco with the bogie removed, in about 1930. *G. Coltas*

18
View from the 'Birdcage'. 'Q4' No 63201, fresh from overhaul at Gorton Tank, runs along the down slow line. A good section of the Works frontage can be seen, and in the foreground are the up and down main lines. *W. A. Brown*

Part Two: The Passenger Scene
4 Going 'B17'

When No 2834 *Hinchingbrooke* was allocated brand-new to Gorton in June 1931, joining No 2816 *Fallodon*, this was the first time that two 'B17' engines had ever been based in Manchester at the same time, although of course No 2816 and its predecessors had been working the North Country Continental for some time past. The spare 'B17' could now be diagrammed for native GC turns, although when this process came into effect has not been ascertained, as there is a certain amount of mystery as to where No 2834 was operating from at the very beginning of its career. Though officially posted to Gorton on 17 June, it was reported working on Doncaster turns in the weeks immediately following, one of the sources being the contemporary *Railway Magazine*. The most probable explanation is that, although officially attached to Gorton, it was run-in at Doncaster and thus came to be used on certain turns operated by that shed; among these was a working to Banbury via Tuxford, Kirkby South Junction and the GC line, and thus it is quite likely that the first 'B17' seen south of Sheffield was actually working from Doncaster.

So far as can be discovered, No 2834 moved to Gorton during the following month. An observer who visited the shed during July noted No 2834 in the vicinity, and was told that it had been sent to Manchester to be used on the through workings to London. A subsequent issue of the RCTS *Railway Observer* reported that the engine had worked two trial trips from Manchester to London, though no precise date is given. It seems likely that these trips coincided with the observations mentioned, and as the engine made only two trips and was not noted subsequently it is to be presumed that, for some reason, it was not required on the London jobs. A possible explanation is that, if the spare 'B17' was to be used as a covering engine for the 'Continental', it obviously could not be allowed to remain overnight in London. Such a decision would explain why at this period both *Hinchingbrooke* and *Fallodon* were absent from Top Link work, and were used instead in the No 2 Link; both were photographed on what are clearly the latter at about this time.

It is interesting however that the 'B17s' should have been bracketed in a link with engines such as the 'Sam Fays', which hints at something of a come-down for a modern type of locomotive, and we should at this point consider the fact that, whatever its true capabilities, the 'B17' was an extremely unpopular engine at Gorton. The Manchester enginemen were very parochial in their outlook, as were most people brought up in the atmosphere of the pre-Grouping companies, and long before the 'B17' design had appeared there had developed a keen dislike of Doncaster products. GC men based in the north-west had had ample opportunities of sizing up Great Northern locomotives because of the regular appearance of 'K2' and 'J6' engines on the goods turns from Nottingham, not to mention the Pacifics and 'K3s' stationed at Gorton not long after Grouping, and they greatly disliked what they saw. The general criticisms were flimsiness of construction, rough riding, lack of cab comfort, awkward controls, and in some instances inadequate power. The arrival of No 2802 *Walsingham* at the end of 1928 had done nothing to alter these opinions; it was claimed that the engine was flimsily built, vibrated badly at speed, and lacked power in the upper speed ranges; there are also well-authenticated eye-witness reports that the type was prone to slip when starting. So the relegation of Nos 2816 and 2834 to No 2 Link duties was probably greeted with relief, especially by the firemen as they would not have relished the prospect of firing through to London on the bucking footplate, and working 'left-handed' because of the altered driving position.

Whilst No 2834 was settling in at Gorton, Nos 2832/3/5 were doing the same at Doncaster, having arrived there new. They were diagrammed mainly to two turns, the Banbury working already mentioned, and a triangular job involving Doncaster-York-Hull-Doncaster; of these, the former demanded considerably harder work for both engine and men. Both of these diagrams included goods workings, and it is curious that although the 'B17s' could hardly be described as mixed traffic engines, the three Doncaster representatives put in about half of their time on goods work. This is all the more unusual when it is remembered that there were numerous 'K2' and 'K3' engines at Doncaster, both types eminently suitable for mixed traffic work.

The Banbury job was worked by Doncaster's volunteer GC link, consisting of men who had transferred in from Mexborough under a reorganisation scheme carried out soon after Grouping. Though they were sometimes teamed with former GN firemen, the drivers were purely GC in upbringing, and thus fully accustomed to such non-GN practices as regular lodging; the Banbury turn also involved night work, as the outward trip was on the 8.17pm fitted fish ex-Decoy Yard. This was worked along the GN main line as far as the junction at Tuxford, then via the LDEC route to Nottingham and finally to Banbury by means of the junction off the GC just south of Woodford. Having handed their train over to the GWR, the men went back light engine to Woodford where they booked off duty. The return working for the engine, now in the charge of a different crew, was the 7.42pm ex-Banbury, the well-known Penzance-Aberdeen express passenger train, and probably it was the nature of this working which dictated the use of 'B17s', although in fact 'K3s' had worked the train perfectly satisfactorily in the past, and were to do so in the future despite a notice in the working timetables to the effect that Class B17 engines must be regularly provided for the Banbury job. The men who had come up with the overnight fish went home earlier in the day, usually on a goods to Sheffield, as the 7.42pm train would have entailed too long a stop-over at Woodford. The arrangement whereby the Doncaster 'B17' spent the better part of 18 hours standing on Woodford Loco does not seem to have been a particularly economical piece of working, and with the mandatory use of 'B17s' the Banbury turn seemed to possess something of a makeshift quality.

From a GC point of view the importance of the turn was that for the first time the new 4-6-0s worked regularly south of Leicester, this being the territorial limit of the Gorton-based engines. Observers in the south Midlands thus had the opportunity of witnessing the by no means displeasing spectacle of a 'B17' in full cry with an express passenger train, even though only in the down direction. However, as already hinted the class never came to dominate the Penzance-Aberdeen train in the way they did the 'Continental', for example. They did not appear on Mondays because there was no outward working from Doncaster on the Sunday evening, and even during the other days of the week their appearances were not invariable, although precise dates are lacking apart from a diary kept during 1937. On 23 March the train was worked by 'K3' No 2498 which had come up overnight on the 10pm 'Scotch Goods' from York, and on the following Thursday by No 4453, a Doncaster Atlantic. On 14 and 16 April the engines were No 2833 *Kimbolton Castle* and 'K3' No 2764. All these appearances, it should be remembered, took place at a time when according to the working timetables the diagram was to be worked by nothing other than a 'B17' engine.

It was something of a departure from the best GC practice for the engine to be worked by a different crew in each direction, and this suggests that the turn was not to be classed with the cream of GC workings. There was even a rather slapdash quality about the concluding stage of the return trip, for the engine came off at Sheffield Victoria and reached Doncaster by assisting a stopping train, a somewhat unusual finish to the journey.

It is interesting that at Doncaster Loco the 'B17s' were always known as 'Castles'. This nickname probably arose because the first two of the class to go there were named *Belvoir Castle* and *Kimbolton Castle*, but it may also point to a rumour current at the time that the 'B17s' had been designed as a result of the impact made by the GWR 'Castle' engine during the exchange of 1925.

From the spring of 1931 and throughout the following year the situation regarding 'B17s' on the GC remained the same. The principal London turns were firmly in the hands of Gorton-designed engines, and the new 4-6-0s were thus unknown at Marylebone. A brief exception to this rule occurred during Christmas week of 1932 when No 2823 *Lambton Castle*, temporarily stationed at Doncaster because of repairs to the regular 'B17s', took out the 10.5pm Mail; the *Railway Observer* described this as 'a fleeting appearance'. It seems that some unusual workings were in operation at the time because the 'B17' is reported to have worked right through to Manchester

on the Mail, instead of engines being changed at Leicester as was normally the case. This may have come about because of heavy traffic during the Christmas period, and the mail train referred to could have been a duplicate. It is likely that No 2823 reached London after working to Banbury on one of the up goods or fish trains, for it sometimes happened that engines which had reached Woodford by this means did not have a direct return working, and were sent to Marylebone to assist on the Mail, which was often quite heavy.

The real revolution in GC fast passenger working came at the beginning of June 1933, when 'B17s' Nos 2840/1/2 were sent to Gorton after a short spell of running-in at Doncaster. The story of this development begins, strangely enough, at Stratford Works in the previous year, when Edward Thompson brought out the first of his series of 'B12' rebuilds, No 8579. This engine was an immediate success. Not only was it found capable of doing anything a 'B17' could do, but it had the advantage of being more popular with the GE footplatemen than the latter, the men's attitude being somewhat similar to that of their confreres at Gorton. Further rebuilds were quickly ordered and another four had been completed by the end of the year. However, before the first rebuilt 'B12' had gone into service a batch of six 'B17s' had been ordered for the GE Section, scheduled to take the rails in the spring of 1933. With five rebuilt 'B12s' on the strength by this time, and a further three to come out very soon, there was insufficient work for the new 'B17s' and the last three were therefore redirected to Gorton, where it was anticipated that more suitable employment could be found for them.

Such a sequence of events helps to explain why these 'B17s' arrived on the GC fitted with the very small GE-type tenders, which held barely enough coal for the arduous London turns. Official capacity was only four tons, which allowed an average consumption of only 40lb per mile for the 206-mile trip to Marylebone. This figure did not include light engine and empty stock working, and the margin thus left little in hand for emergencies.

Despite this, the decision was taken to use the 'B17s' in the Top Link. One argument in its favour was uniformity; because the 'Continental' turn had to be worked by a 'B17' it was necessary for drivers to switch over from their usual 'Director' engine when it came their turn to go to Ipswich, and the presence of a fleet of 'B17s' would eliminate this difficulty. In view of the reputation of the 'B17s' however it is hardly surprising that the new scheme was unpopular. The most noticeable demonstration of this feeling was the refusal of one of the men, Driver J. Rickards, to take out a 'B17' in place of his usual 'Director'. He carried his objection to the point of booking off duty and going home, refusing to co-operate until he was finally allowed to keep his original engine.

No 2840 *Somerleyton Hall* and No 2841 *Gayton Hall* were officially posted to Gorton on 2 June, and both were noted on that day and the next working No 2 Link turns, probably on a trial basis. The earliest record of them working the senior turns is on 15 June, when No 2841 was seen approaching Manchester on the 3.20pm from Marylebone, and if we remember that this was not necessarily the first occasion on which they had worked to London it can be seen that little time was wasted in promoting them to the best jobs. The third engine of the trio, No 2842 *Kilverstone Hall*, reached Gorton on 10 June and soon afterwards worked the Gorton half of the 'Continental' working for a complete week.

Whatever the crews may have thought of them, the 'B17s' brought a touch of the spectacular to the GC. In terms of appearance they have always been somewhat overshadowed by their large cousins the Pacifics, and the fact that none of the class has been preserved tends to make us forget what handsome machines they were. By 1933 the 'Directors' and GC Atlantics which worked so many of the best GC Section trains were painted black, only the small number of 'Sam Fays' and 'Lord Faringdons' remaining green once the economy regulations of 1928 had begun to take effect. Hence the new engines brought a welcome splash of colour to the proceedings, and the condition in which they were kept by the Gorton 'bogie cleaners' was well and truly up to the usual standard. In the realm of sound they brought an entirely new note, in the literal sense of the word, to the usual GC mixture of noises; the scream of the shrill Gresley whistle, so different from the rather flat GC sound, enabled the the engines to advertise their presence for miles around, especially as they made their way over the wild moorland between Penistone and Woodhead. The staccato drumming of the exhaust was equally unmistakable, and the whirling rods produced a clank that was as musical as church bells. Unfortunately these distinctive sounds had been stilled by the time the first consumer-available tape recorders made the preservation of locomotive noises a practical possibility.

The appearance of a 'B17' at the head of a Manchester-Marylebone express was a reliable indication of the presence of Gorton men on the footplate, for strange though it may seem, the allocation of 'B17s' to Gorton was not paralleled by any similar development at Neasden, despite the fact that the London shed shared in the through workings between north and south. Neasden 'Directors' continued to come regularly to Manchester on the 3.20pm down express every Monday, Wednesday and Friday, and to go back each succeeding day with the 2.20 up. This rather lopsided situation offers further evidence of the makeshift planning which lay behind the arrival of the 'B17' engines on the GC.

In day-to-day working however, the use of 'B17s' on Gorton's London jobs was not invariable, partly perhaps because of the attitude adopted by Driver Rickards. On Tuesday 20 June No 5433 *Walter Burgh Gair* worked the 3.20pm from Marylebone, and in the first week of July, No 5503 *Somme* twice worked this turn; another Gorton favourite, No 5438 *Worsley-Taylor*, appeared on it on Tuesday 11 July. It is unlikely that these appearances can be explained by the presence of Jimmy Rickards on the footplate, and the more likely cause is that the regular 'B17' was not available. No 2816 *Fallodon* was under repair at Stratford Works during this

time, and with at least one of the remaining 'B17s' continuously tied up on the 'Continental' working, the pool of engines available for the London jobs was stretched to its limit. To improve this situation another 'B17' was sent to Gorton the following November; this was No 2824 *Lumley Castle*, and with No 2816 now back in traffic Gorton could deploy six of the type for its best workings. This was the precise number of engines which Gorton Works had built on two occasions in the past especially for Top Link workings, the types concerned being the 'Sam Fays' and the 'Lord Faringdons'. Unfortunately *Lumley Castle* turned out to be a particularly disappointing engine, even by 'B17' standards, and was rostered only on very rare occasions for the London turns. A likely explanation for its transfer from the GE Section is that the growing numbers of rebuilt 'B12s' furnished an opportunity for less satisfactory 'B17s' to be got rid of. The engine seems to have preserved its poor record right to the end, as it was the first of the class to be withdrawn in 1952.

There is also evidence that by the end of 1933 the use of 'B17s' on the best work was declining, despite the increase in numbers. Whether this was a result of the attitude adopted by the footplatemen, or came about because of the engines running short of coal on the long runs is impossible to say. Records show that the 'Directors' were beginning to take an increasingly prominent part in the workings again, and by June 1934, 12 months after their debut, the 'B17s' were playing a definite second fiddle. Notes of engine working on the 2.20 up and 3.20 down expresses have been traced for the whole of that month, and show that out of a total of 24 journeys performed by Gorton engines and men between 4 and 30 June, only 10 were entrusted to 'B17s'; of these, six came in the final week when No 2816 ran the whole of the Gorton working unchanged, this engine being one of the more popular 'B17s' until it fell on hard times early in 1936. As a contrast to the poor 'B17' record, the amazing No 5505 *Ypres* of Neasden did 14 round trips, including two complete weeks.

The limited coal capacity of the GE-type tenders has already been mentioned, and special care had to be taken to get as much on them as possible to avoid the risk of running short en route. The following extract gives some indication of the special attention that was devoted to this task; it was written by the late Frank Rushton, who was a cleaner at Gorton at about 1933:

'The "B17" tenders were stacked up with large lumps of coal at the front and sides, and piled up to the height of the cab top if the driver considered it necessary. After the fire was built up, and I mean cobbed up, the driver would then go for another tub or two of coal to top up the tender again. But they seemed to manage the "Continental" all right. I remember when cleaning for Algy Roberts and Harry Toft on No 2816 *Fallodon*; we the cleaners built the fire up and we used to pinch large lumps off other tenders on to the footplate while your mate piled them into the firebox. Harry Toft used to tell us that on arriving at Bury St Edmunds the plate on the tender box was taken out and he was scratching coal from the back of the tender, but they managed.

'When the coal hopper was in operation the stacking was the same — put a bit on, pick the lumps out for stacking, then have another go until it was stacked high, although the lumps were smaller. If extra coal was necessary, the man had assistance to take the engine via the engine line at the wet ashpit to the hopper for topping up . . .

'The same applied for the London and Ipswich jobs. Not much was left on these small tenders.'

It was in 1934 that some degree of recovery from the depression became evident in traffics, and during the summer season there was an increase in the loading of certain trains, particularly at weekends. In an effort to recover business lost to road transport, a change in ticket availability was put into effect whereby passengers travelling on excursion tickets were free to make return journeys by the regular services if they preferred, instead of being restricted to excursion trains. This move seems to have been successful inasmuch as the loading of some of the regular trains began to increase considerably. One of them was the 3.20pm down, and in order to preserve its reputation for punctuality it became necessary to make use of an assistant engine, a practice hitherto unknown on the Manchester-London trains, and seldom adopted anywhere on the GC. A new Saturday diagram was introduced at Neasden whereby an engine was turned out to assist the 3.20 down, travelling as far as Leicester and then coming off to await return on the 3.50pm Manchester-Marylebone express, which left Leicester at 6.44. The type used was normally a 'D10' and was attached regardless of whether the train engine was a 'Director' or a 'B17', though it should be noted that under the arrangements originally introduced in 1933 the train would normally have been headed by one of the latter as this was a Gorton return working. This shows clearly that the 'B17s' were not considered to be much superior to the older engines in terms of power.

The continuing use of 'Directors' was no doubt partly a result of the men's long experience of the type, and willingness to get the very best out of them; one notable feature of the 1934 summer workings was the contribution made by Gorton's No 5433 *Walter Burgh Gair*, clearly a great favourite in Manchester and obviously well able to do the work. It appeared frequently on the Saturday down working, despite being over 20 years old by this date. Of Neasden's 'Directors', No 5505 *Ypres* has already been mentioned as putting in some good work, and at one period it ran the through Manchester turn four consecutive weeks without a break, an amazing performance. Work of this kind, it should be added, was achieved on a much superior maintenance record to that of the 'B17s', which were considerably more frequent in their visits to the shops.

The next move in the history of the GC-based 'B17s' is a curious one, the reason for which can only be suggested. At the close of 1934 three of the Gorton engines were transferred to Neasden, these being Nos 2834, 2842 and,

almost inevitably, the iniquitous 2824. In exchange, 'B3s' Nos 6164/5/7 came north to balance up the numbers. The latter had worked regularly on Neasden's well-known night jobs, the 'Mail' and the 'Newspaper', and it appears that the 'B17s' took their place, working these jobs to Leicester and back. We have no record of how they fared on these heavy and exacting turns, and one wonders how the Neasden men felt about tackling the notorious 'Newspaper' working with No 2824 *Lumley Castle*. The trio remained at Neasden for almost exactly 12 months and then came back to Gorton in the same abrupt manner as they had departed.

It is possible that this rather unusual move may have been made in order to give the London men some opportunity of handling the 'B17s', as it was during March 1935 that the first batch of the new 'B17' 'Footballers' were ordered for general service on the GC Section. Likewise, their utilisation on a different range of workings would have provided useful information. On the other hand, the move to Neasden may have been simply an attempt to find a fresh sphere of activity for the engines as a result of their apparently declining utilisation in Manchester. If the latter was the case, then the return of the engines to the north suggests that the idea had not borne fruit, and it is certainly very doubtful whether the 'B17s' enhanced their reputation in any way as a result of the move. The prejudices which had such a strong hold at Gorton were equally in evidence at the southern end of the line, and in addition the Neasden passenger men had always been used to receiving newly-built engines to do the top-flight jobs. The reception which they must have given to the 'B17s', one of them already rejected, it seemed, both at Gorton and on the GE Section, would hardly conduce to enthusiastic operation of the engines. Perhaps the most significant detail is that the extensive records of through workings to Manchester do not yield a single instance of the Neasden 'B17s' ever being used on this turn during the whole of 1935.

With only three 'B17s' remaining at Gorton during that year, of which No 2841 had two spells in Gorton shops in that time, the position of pre-1933 was largely reverted to, with one of the engines regularly working the 'Continental' and the others kept in Manchester in reserve. So there are few appearances of the Class to be placed on record during 1935 as far as the London turns are concerned, and the 'Director's once more dominated the scene.

The Gorton works staff made the acquaintance of the 'B17s' in November 1934, when as a result of official instructions the work of carrying out general overhauls to the class was transferred from Stratford. Reports indicate that the men did not enjoy working on them; stripping them down was considered a particularly arduous job, mainly because the constant vibration caused nuts to become distorted and frequently seized. Worse than this was the difficulty of getting them back into satisfactory running order after reassembly, as they often had to return more than once to the shops for adjustment even though officially returned to traffic. Some allowance ought perhaps to be made here for the same kind of local prejudice as influenced the footplatemen, but it is interesting that similar complaints were apparently made on the GE Section during the 1950s. Some engines seem to have had especially poor availability records, for example No 2816 *Fallodon* which was repaired at the end of 1935, was found unsuitable for Top Link work until it had revisited the shops in May 1936, and then after eight months of normal use was in the shops again from March until the middle of November 1937. The generally poor maintenance figures contrast with the painstaking care and attention which the engines received in daily service. To quote Frank Rushton again: 'All fast train engines had their fires dropped, and before lighting up the boiler-makers used to examine the firebox. Fires were never kept in for these jobs.' In addition to this, the engines used by Gorton and Neasden on the long-distance turns were always carefully set aside at the end of each trip, usually berthed on a special road, and were never used on 'fill-in' workings; Sunday was treated as a 'rest day' and gave the shed fitters an opportunity to rectify minor defects. This high standard of maintenance reflects clearly in the availability record of the 'Directors', some of which were in the shops only half a dozen times between 1930 and the outbreak of war. The best record, almost inevitably, was that achieved by No 5505 *Ypres* — five general repairs, totalling only 138 days out of traffic.

The return of the Neasden trio to Gorton at the beginning of 1936 brought further appearances on the London turns, but once again the 'Directors' were not fully ousted. In mid-February No 5501 *Mons* did a full week of London work, and No 5508 *Prince of Wales* likewise during the last week of March.

The subject of names may be mentioned as a postscript. The series of names bestowed on the original 'B17s' undoubtedly produced some very pleasant-sounding titles, highly suitable for fast passenger loco-motives. However on the GC some of them were mis-rendered in a manner somewhat characteristic of working men's gritty sense of humour. *Hinchingbrooke* was usually referred to as 'Itchin Brook', and the name *Walsingham* was thought appropriate because of the rough riding characteristics — 'waltzing 'em'. *Quidenham*, the name of one of the first 'B17s' to work on the 'Continental' turn, sparked off witticisms about the wealth accumulated by Top Link drivers, ever a popular topic of conversation. At Doncaster the name *Milton* occasioned some remark as it was the brand-name of a household antiseptic much used between the wars.

From mid-1936 however such jokes began to be a thing of the past, for as recorded in the next chapter the earlier 'B17s' were mostly to be eliminated from the GC Section by the influx of what were officially designated Class B17/4, but were much better known to both staff and lineside observers as 'Footballers'.

19
A view taken during the first flowering of 'B17' through running to London. No 2834 *Hinchingbrooke* backs off Gorton Loco on Sunday 30 July 1933 for the 4.50pm departure from Sheffield, thence forward to Marylebone; the pile of coal on the tender will be noted. Sleepers and rails are seen ready for relaying in connection with demolition of the coal stage. *G. Coltas*

20
No 2834 *Hinchingbrooke* again, this time on the 2.20pm
Manchester-Marylebone express at Nottingham Victoria on
28 August 1937. The work of the Gorton 'bogie cleaners' is
very much in evidence.
T. G. Hepburn/Rail Archive Stephenson

21
In the high summer of 'B17' working. No 2840 *Somerleyton
Hall* of Gorton is on an unidentified down express at
Bagthorpe Junction about 1933.
T. G. Hepburn/Rail Archive Stephenson

22
Saturday double-heading. The 'Sam Fay' down approaches
Harrow-on-the-Hill with Gorton's No 2816 *Fallodon* and 'C4'
No 6085 in the summer of 1935.
T. G. Hepburn/Rail Archive Stephenson

21

23
The reign of the 'Directors'. 'D11' No 5501 *Mons* emerges
from Mansfield Road tunnel into Nottingham Victoria with
an up express in the 1930s. 'B3' No 6164 *Earl Beatty* stands
by after working a special, probably from Marylebone.
T. G. Hepburn/Rail Archive Stephenson

24
No 2816 *Fallodon* pulls out of Chorlton-cum-Hardy station
with a Manchester-Central-Guide Bridge evening local in
June 1934. *W. Potter*

25

25
No 2802 *Walsingham* was Gorton's first 'B17', arriving new in 1928 for service on the 'North Country Continental'. It is seen here on a down express at Nottingham Victoria, probably in 1929.
T. G. Hepburn/Rail Archive Stephenson

26
Neasden's No 5506 *Butler-Henderson* at Amersham, working home after going out with the 10am Marylebone-Bradford express. Leaning out of the cab is Driver Fred France, who was originally a Gorton man; he fired on the first trial coaching train from Manchester to Marylebone, and on the first booked passenger train from Manchester to Marylebone on 15 March 1899. *R. H. N. Hardy*

27

27
No 5433 *Walter Burgh Gair* was without doubt Gorton's best 'D10'. It is seen here approaching Marylebone in the later 1920s, while allocated to Neasden. *Real Photographs*

28
The remarkable No 5505 *Ypres* is at Charwelton with an up stopping train on 3 July 1937; in those days the name was probably pronounced 'Wipers' as on the Western Front in 1914-18. *L. Hanson*

28

29
An immaculate No 2835 *Milton* is seen at Banbury whilst employed on one of Doncaster's lodging turns to Woodford. Fireman Hector Quince of Doncaster is seen on the footplate. *Photomatic*

30
No 2834 *Hinchingbrooke* climbs out of Nottingham with the 12.15pm Marylebone-Manchester express about 1932. The building at left is the New Basford carriage shed.
T. G. Hepburn/Rail Archive Stephenson

5 The 'Footballer' Interlude

No 2848 *Arsenal*, first of the 'Footballers', arrived on the GC Section on or about Tuesday 3 March 1936, and things happened quickly after that. By the end of June a further 13 had appeared on the scene, making a major impact on the services. A second very concentrated dose was administered in the following year, with another 11 engines being drafted in between February and July. The whole sequence completed a revolution in GC Section passenger working the like of which had never been seen before.

The arrival en bloc of so many 'Footballers' contrasts markedly with the somewhat half-hearted moves described in earlier chapters, and such a comprehensive programme of re-equipment points to a definite decision having been made with regard to the employment of 'B17s'. This decision, we are to presume, was made early in 1935 when the first batch of 'Footballers' was ordered, and it would seem that the management had finally settled on the 'B17' as a suitable type of engine for the GC Section passenger services. However it is interesting that the new engines were allowed to operate widely on the GE Section, a list of permitted routes being published in 1935, quite some time before the first of the series was built, and this fact together with the later replacement of the 'Footballers' by larger engines, as recounted in the next chapter, has led to a suggestion that they were intended to be used only temporarily on the GC until larger engines were available. This is in some ways a not unattractive idea, but the authors incline to the view that in spite of later developments there is considerable evidence that an effort was being made to have the 'B17s' adopted as a 'standard class', with wide use being canvassed for them in the Southern and North Eastern Areas. The scheme seems to have foundered on strong opposition from the NE Area management, but got far enough to ensure a plentiful supply of 'B17s' for the GC.

Rumours as to what sort of engine was to appear had been circulating among the staff for some time prior to the emergence of No 2848, and when speculation was finally set at rest there was a certain disappointment. An impression had gained ground that a considerably improved type of engine was to be brought out, and there was a corresponding reaction when the 'new type' turned out to be nothing more than the same old 'B17' coupled to a bigger tender. The prospect of working on this type of locomotive meant no respite from the regular shaking which was a part of daily life for 'B17' crews, and indeed many men with experience of the type have claimed that the 'Footballers' were worse than the originals in this respect.

The only other difference, not of much relevance from a footplateman's point of view but of great interest nonetheless, was the adoption of a new naming series. The decision to name locomotives after Association Football clubs may not have been to everyone's taste, but it was a stroke which showed the LNER flair for publicity at its best. Over the years the proximity of Wembley Stadium to GC metals had resulted in a steady flow of special traffic connected with Association Football, and particularly with the FA Cup Final. The new names thus drew attention to an important and somewhat unique aspect of GC Section passenger working. Three of the four Cup semi-finalists of 1936 were clubs whose grounds were directly accessible by LNER metals, and having won their respective ties a few days before the appearance of No 2848, they became the first of the new series. They were Arsenal, Sheffield United and Grimsby Town; all were old and distinguished clubs, but in the year of grace 1936 Arsenal could claim to be by far the most famous of the three, thanks to a remarkable run of success which gave them undisputed claim to be considered the team of the decade. They were also, it need hardly be added, odds-on favourites to win the Cup, and so they received the honour of being put first. They duly returned the compliment a few weeks later by fulfilling the forecasts.

Several of the new names were bestowed to the accompaniment of special ceremonies, which gave a further publicity boost. The practice of holding naming ceremonies had suddenly come into fashion, it seems, with the naming of an earlier 'B17', No 2845 *The Suffolk Regiment*, at Ipswich in the previous year, and this new custom was to be made much use of by the LNER in the years leading up to the war. A gathering of Arsenal FC players and officials was present at Kings Cross for the naming of No 2848, the ceremony being performed by a well-known sportsman, the club Chairman Lord Lonsdale. Sometimes the ceremonies were held during the public exhibitions of LNER rolling stock which were another popular feature of the period.

To add still further to the impact made by these engines, the centre splashers carried a cast half-section of a football, and were embellished on either side with panels displaying the club colours. These colours were painted to correspond fairly closely with the actual style of shirt worn on the field, and thus the all-red panels of No 2848 were followed by vertical red and white stripes on No 2849 *Sheffield United*, black and white stripes for No 2850 *Grimsby Town*, and so on. There were even horizontal stripes to represent the hoops worn by Darlington and Doncaster Rovers. Compared with what was happening on such staid railways as the SR and GWR it was all very novel.

With such eye-catching features, and the more harmonious LNER tender replacing the short GC type, the 'Footballers' have generally been regarded as more attractive machines than those of the earlier series.

Further publicity could also be obtained, of course, by rostering the engines to work specials conveying supporters of the particular clubs, and such opportunities were frequently made use of. No 2849 was used to work a Cup Final special from Sheffield on 25 April, the day Sheffield United faced the ultimately victorious Arsenal at

Wembley; when Sunderland appeared in the 1937 Final, the LNER even went to the trouble of doing a switch of name and number with another engine when it was found that No 2854 *Sunderland* was out of traffic for repairs, and a few weeks before this the newly-named No 2862 *Manchester United* had been used to work football specials from Manchester Central to the stadium station at Old Trafford, even though the occasion was nothing more exceptional than a League match with Brentford.

So far as day-to-day running was concerned, the first shed to feel the impact of the 'Footballer' invasion was Leicester, which received Nos 2848-55 during March and April. This was a not unexpected manoeuvre, as the Class C4 Atlantics which they replaced there were by this time 30 years old. These wonderful GC veterans had done yeoman service at Leicester, having become almost synonymous with that shed from the time of Grouping; their replacement on the principal services was undoubtedly a blow to the men in the senior links, for most of the drivers could claim to have grown up with the class. It has to be said however that there had been increasing evidence of the engines' inability to cope with some of the harder turns, several of which were now more difficult than in the past. The gradual rise in trainloads has already been mentioned in the previous chapter, and Leicester felt the effects of this as much as other sheds, or perhaps even more on account of the large number of passenger diagrams which they operated. In addition, the very difficult 6.20pm down Bradford express was made an even more formidable assignment by the withdrawal of the slip carriages and substitution of stops at Finmere and Woodford. There was thus a need for a more modern engine at Leicester by 1936 if not before, and whatever may have been the feelings of the men towards the 'Footballers' they must have realised that a change was considerably overdue. It is interesting to relate that the anti-'B17' feeling which was so noticeable at both ends of the GC main line does not seem to have had such a hold at Leicester, and the indications are that the men settled down to do some very good work with them; there is certainly little doubt that Leicester became the best 'B17 shed' on the GC, although the men were under no illusions about the riding qualities of the 4-6-0s compared with the rock-steady Atlantics.

The Leicester engines enjoyed a wide sphere of operations, covering the whole of the GC line between Manchester and Marylebone, and thus they quickly advertised their presence over the whole system. They were considerably more common south of Sheffield, working a mixture of Manchester and Bradford expresses together with a few turns on the north-to-west trains. With all eight engines going into traffic in as many weeks, it must have seemed to observers on this part of the GC that an LNER take-over was in progress.

The remaining six engines of the first batch were divided evenly between Gorton and Neasden, the last of the order reaching Gorton at the end of June. With the arrival of the three newcomers the total of 'B17s' based in Manchester rose to nine, which was more than enough to cover the principal workings; as a result three of the well-

loved 'Directors' were transferred away, an event which marked the end of an era at Gorton. The swansong of the mighty 'D11s' seems to have come early in the following September, when No 5511 *Marne* worked a full week on the Manchester-London turns. At Neasden the new arrivals displaced two 'Directors', and an event of some importance was the appearance on 10 July of No 2856 *Leeds United* on the through Manchester turn, this being almost certainly the first time that the London men had preferred the newer engines to the 'D11s'. Soon afterwards No 2857 *Doncaster Rovers* began to appear quite regularly, and it was apparent that times were changing.

The Gorton 'Footballers' were put to early use on the 'Continental', for contrary to what has often been stated in the past they were permitted over virtually all GE Section routes open to the original engines. The first of the series to have the distinction of working to Ipswich was No 2859 *Norwich City* in the week beginning 6 July, and from this time onwards 'Footballers' were regularly used on the turn.

Delivery of the second batch of 'Footballers' commenced in mid-January 1937 with the allocation of No 2862 to Gorton. On 12 February this engine was officially named *Manchester United* in the course of a ceremony at Manchester Central Station, with the city's Lord Mayor and the club Chairman both present. On the footplate were Driver Jack Glover and Fireman Sam Cunliffe of Gorton, the former already a veteran of the express passenger workings. The engine made its debut in the Top Link when it worked to Ipswich with the 'Continental' the following Monday.

Most of this latter batch went to swell the existing allocations at Gorton and Leicester, but in addition three engines were sent to Sheffield and two to Woodford. The class were now represented at all the main sheds on the Manchester-London line and by the summer of 1937 the impact of the 'Footballers' on GC services was at its greatest, with every engine based somewhere between Manchester and Marylebone. They had a complete monopoly of the Manchester-London service apart from the overnight trains, and worked most of the expresses south of Leicester, although here they still had some competition from Neasden's 'Directors' and 'Lord Faringdons', which had not been entirely ousted from the best turns. Their only other rivals were the GN Atlantics operated so successfully from Sheffield Loco, although these were restricted to the Sheffield-Leicester section and the Hull-Liverpool expresses.

Sheffield's three 'B17s' stayed only a year, and during that time did not supplant the outstandingly popular Atlantics on the difficult Woodhead workings. They were used mainly on the turns to Leicester and back, and apart from this their chief responsibility was the long-distance working to Swindon shared on a periodic basis with the GWR and routed via Banbury. This job involved lodging at Swindon Loco, surely the most unlikely spot ever reached by the 'Footballers' in normal service. The solitary 'B17' must have looked decidedly out of place surrounded by a host of Great Western engines, and one wonders what sort of remarks the local men passed about the visitor with its unusual half-section football and coloured panels. It was on this working that Driver Charlie Skelton put up such an excellent performance with No 2863 *Everton* by outdoing the schedule of the famous 'Cheltenham Flyer' on the stretch between Swindon and Steventon.

The two Woodford engines, Nos 2866/7, were used on the west-to-north expresses between Banbury and Sheffield, but did not remain at the shed very long, being transferred within a few weeks to Neasden and Leicester respectively. They were replaced by Nos 2850/5 and 2847 *Helmingham Hall*.

The widespread introduction of 'Footballers' coincided with yet another change, less apparent but considerably more important. The period between late 1936 and the summer of 1937 saw major changes in the diagramming of GC Section passenger engines, this being part of an LNER economy programme aimed at securing more efficient use of locomotives. The first round of changes came in December 1936, followed by another reshuffle in the succeeding April. Some of the new diagrams were very intensive, and when coupled with the still rising loads of many passenger trains they presented a difficult task from the locomotive point of view. A further important factor was the increasing resort to double or triple manning of engines, necessary in order to keep them at work for longer periods. Such practices inevitably militate against the high standard of care and vigilance which is probably the best feature of single-crewing, and the new arrangements constituted a divergence from traditional GC practice. As an example, the engine of the down 'Continental' was diagrammed to Leicester and back after reaching Manchester, and thus passed through the hands of three separate crews in the course of a working that kept it on the road for over 18 hours.

Under such conditions even the best of locomotives is certain to deteriorate fairly quickly and to become more prone to failure. So presumably it was with this in mind that the Loco Running Department arranged for the changes to be made at a time when more modern engines were available for the new turns. But the growing difficulty of some of the work was to overtax the 'B17s', and to reveal weaknesses which under less exacting conditions might not have mattered so much.

Some examples of the increased loading may convey a more precise picture of what was happening. The 7.30am Sheffield-Marylebone express was mentioned in the *Railway Magazine* of January 1937 as loading regularly to 10 vehicles or more; in the coaching stock diagrams of 1935 this train is shown as a six-coach formation, so that the increase in size and weight was in the order of 66% in the space of 12 months. Similar instances were noted in respect of the 8.20am Manchester-Marylebone and 10am Bradford-Marylebone trains. The 7.30am express was worked throughout by Leicester Loco, which meant that the other two similarly south of Leicester Central, which meant that this work was entrusted entirely to 'B17s'. The return working of the 10am up Bradford diagram was the formidable 6.20pm down, already described.

A very interesting and in some ways more significant example was the 5.30 Sunday evening train from Marylebone to Manchester. This had begun to load up very heavily and by the summer of 1937, if not before, it had acquired a reputation for running late — a thing almost unheard of on the GC. It was worked throughout by a Gorton engine which from April onwards had been operating on a somewhat more intensive diagram than the long-distance engines had worked under the original long-standing arrangements. The lateness appears to have been attributable to the locomotive, which on this long run was plainly being taxed beyond its limit with loads of 10 coaches or more; sometimes further coaches were attached at Sheffield to make the load even heavier for the last punishing climb to Woodhead.

Despite these substantial increases in load, very little was done in the way of easing the schedules of GC expresses, which it should be remembered were still basically the same as in the days when the trains consisted of only four or five vehicles. Only in a very few cases was extra time added, and this never amounted to more than two or three minutes.

An insertion in the *Railway Magazine* of October 1937 drew attention to the difficulty of working certain trains, and reported some instances of double-heading. Such practices were not of course quite as novel as the wording suggested, because as mentioned in the previous chapter there had been regular double-heading of the 3.20 down and 3.50 up Marylebone trains as early as three years before, even though only at weekends. It seems unlikely however that news of this would have taken so long to reach the *Railway Magazine*, and the announcement probably referred to more general use of piloting, although the absence of detail makes the reference very obscure. By the time this news got into print however it had become evident that in respect of certain trains the 'Footballers' were being asked to do more than they were capable of; they were after all only moderately dimensioned machines, and as has been suggested in the previous chapter, probably not a great advance on the 'Directors'. Furthermore they had not been designed for the GC routes and stood up badly to the punishment they received on the curves and gradients. Even during 1936 when they were still new, no fewer than six of the 'Footballers' had to go into Gorton Works for short spells; Nos 2849/60 went in twice, and No 2850 was there for most of September. Some of these engines made further visits in the following year, notably No 2860 which was out of traffic for another two months, and No 2849; by the end of the year these two had been in the works three times since first going into traffic. In 1938 No 2866 was repaired three times between February and December, spending over three months out of traffic. Darlington had repaired No 2861 twice at the end of 1936, keeping it out of action for over three months. Other examples could be readily quoted. The availability record of the 'Footballers' was clearly much below that achieved by Gorton-designed engines on comparable work, and we remind readers again of the example of 'D11' No 5505 — five repairs in little short of 10 years, and a total of less than five months spent out of traffic.

It is usual for the designer to take most of the blame when engines perform poorly, but in this instance such criticism hardly seems to be justified. The 'B17' design had been evolved by Nigel Gresley back in 1927-8 to meet restrictions on the GE Section which were not encountered elsewhere, and the distinguished designer could not at that time have been expected to know that nearly 10 years later the engines would be used on an entirely different part of LNER. Nor would it be fair to criticise the footplatemen, who although they never liked the engines obviously did the best they could in the circumstances. If there is blame to be apportioned, this belongs to those elements in the management who were advocating wide use of the 'B17s'. With piloting of the engines already a regular occurrence on the GC Section by 1934, and trainloads rising, the decision to build more of the type for use on the GC is certainly open to criticism.

The fact that the 'Footballers' have not been much criticised in the past probably stems from the writings of the late C. J. Allen. His opinions of locomotive performance never failed to carry a great deal of weight, and in two *Railway Magazine* articles published in July 1936 and April 1937 he hailed them as a major advance in GC Section power. His views were based on what were undoubtedly excellent runs between Leicester and Marylebone, the details clearly showing the extent to which they were superior to the GC Atlantics they had recently replaced at Leicester.

The main objection to his assessment is that it was based on what is clearly a very restricted and unrepresentative sample of information. The section between Leicester and Marylebone was much the easier part of the GC, as has been pointed out in an earlier chapter, and as a general rule Mr Allen seems to have selected for his logs only engines which were setting off fresh at the beginning of a diagram, or at any rate these are the kind of logs which he seems to have published in respect of the 'Footballers'. It would have been interesting to see the sort of results he might have obtained if instead of boarding a train at Leicester headed by an engine fresh from the nearby shed, he had ridden on the 2.20pm from Manchester, where the engine was working through, or gone north on the 3.20 down, where the hardest part of the run was yet to come. In such instances it is likely that he would have recorded some rather different figures from those which appear in the *Railway Magazine*. By comparison with the work done on a through working between Manchester and Marylebone, a single trip from Leicester is not really a true indication of what was expected of the engines on the GC, though this is not of course to take away the credit for what was achieved by the men involved in these published trips.

In the *Railway Magazine* of July 1939 Mr Allen turned his attention to the northern end of the GC line, publishing some logs showing the working of 'Footballers' over Woodhead. These are of the greatest interest, but unfortunately they do not include any timings on the through working from London, and so are subject to the objections already mentioned; they are discussed in more detail in Chapter 8.

Mr Allen was regularly in receipt of logs from other recorders, and a number of his correspondents are known to have timed the 2.20 up and 3.20 down trains over Woodhead during this period, and particularly the latter. It is probable that at least some of these logs were sent to Mr Allen, but none ever appeared in print. It was his usual practice to publish logs which showed high speeds or revealed exceptional haulage capacity, and so the absence of the above logs from his articles seems somewhat indicative.

The *Railway Magazine* announcement dealing with double-heading also carried news of the proposed installation of 70ft turntables at Marylebone and Leicester. These had been ordered in the previous August, and the decision meant in effect the end of the road for the 'Footballers' as far as the principal GC services were concerned. As the next chapter records, they were to disappear fairly steadily from the through workings from September 1938, apart from occasional use as covering engines, and were systematically supplanted on most of the other services from the spring of 1939.

These changes created a situation which was in some ways not dissimilar to that of 10 years before. The first 'B17s', it will be recalled, came to the GC to work the Continental turn, and by the summer of 1939 a position was fast being reached whereby this job was the only important one for which engines of the class were still regularly rostered. Had the war not intervened, it seems probable that the only 'B17s' remaining on the GC would have been the ones needed by Gorton to work this service, for which of course larger engines were not suitable. This would have been in effect a return to the days early in the decade when Nos 2816/34 were at Gorton, their chief responsibility being the 'Continental' turn.

In accordance with the instruction of 1934, described in the previous chapter, the 'Footballers' were scheduled to receive general repairs at Gorton Works, though there were a few isolated exceptions. During 1939 a number of the earlier 'B17s' were repaired at Stratford, as in former times, but the 'Footballers' continued to come to Gorton, even though by this time most of them were on the GE Section. This suggests that the Chief Mechanical Engineer's Department distinguished between the series. The only material difference between the types, apart from the Westinghouse brake fitted to the very early engines, was in the tender type, and the fact that the original series had GE-pattern tenders may possibly have been the reason for the transfer of repair work to Stratford, although in fact a number of 'B17s' with GE tenders were repaired at Gorton during 1939, and No 2806 actually came in for a repair as late as August 1941. It is possible that the repair work was allocated on a basis of available capacity, with the engines being sent to whichever works could deal with them more quickly, but the retention of so much work at Gorton seems curious in view of the distance which the engines had to travel, Stratford obviously being far more convenient for any engine stationed east of Lincoln.

In summing up the achievement of the 'B17s' as far as GC affairs go, it is hardly necessary to say that they gave rather more pleasure to observers than they did to footplate crews. Nevertheless they were on the GC during a very important period of its history, and probably did their best work there. They pioneered some interesting new workings, including turns to Liverpool introduced as a result of the diagram alterations of December 1936, and were the first engines to work the overnight Marylebone-Newcastle trains introduced in 1937; these were inaugurated on 3 May when No 2849 *Sheffield United* took the first train out of Marylebone with Driver Tom Newall of Leicester at the regulator. The workings took GC engines and men north of York for the first time, apart from occasional specials, and introduced the Leicester men to the pleasures of lodging at Gateshead Loco. The 'Footballers' can also claim the distinction of being the only LNER-built engines ever to work regularly to Swindon. Their contribution to the story of GC services is thus an important one, and the only other non-GC class to make a greater impact on what by 1939 had become the Western Section of the Southern Area were the GN Atlantics.

31
No 2862 *Manchester United* on an up train at Staverton Road. First of the Stephenson-built 'B17s', this engine was allocated to Gorton and at first driven regularly by Jack Glover. *G. Coltas*

32
Two months old and still in pristine condition, Gorton's No 2869 *Barnsley* is on the 2.20pm Manchester-Marylebone train at Nottingham Victoria. In the background is Leicester Atlantic No 5360.
T. G. Hepburn/Rail Archive Stephenson

31

32

33
The team of the decade. First of the 'Footballers', No 2848 *Arsenal*, is at Doncaster Carr Loco about 1937.   *G. Coltas*

34
In the heyday of Atlantic working. 'C4' No 5265 was stationed at Leicester for many years in LNER days, and is seen here on its home shed.   *G. Coltas*

35

36

35
'C4' No 6084 leaves Marylebone in about 1931.   *G. Coltas*

36
Only a few months old, No 2865 *Leicester City* poses outside Manchester Central. The football club panels were blue.   *W. Potter*

37
No 2855 *Middlesbrough* has just passed Valehouse on the climb to Woodhead. This is an August 1945 view but nothing has changed from earlier years apart from the appearance of the electrification gantries; the Derbyshire moors loom in the background, and high above the train is 'Devil's Elbow', a notorious bend in the Glossop-Woodhead road.   *W. Potter*

38
No 2857 *Doncaster Rovers* at Neasden Loco in the late 1930s. The football club panels were red and white, painted in horizontal stripes to correspond with the hoops which the team adopted in 1935 following their promotion to Division Two. This view shows off the classic lines of the 'B17s'. *Real Photographs*

38

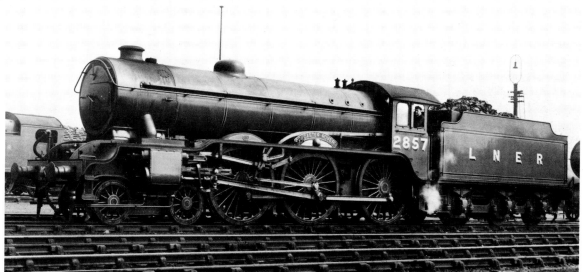

39
No 2850 *Grimsby Town* and 'C4' No 5264, both of
Leicester, are seen at Nottingham Victoria on Sunday
6 August 1939 working the 12.15pm Manchester-
Marylebone train. Once again, the black and white stripes of
Grimsby Town FC are faithfully copied below the nameplate.
T. G. Hepburn/Rail Archive Stephenson

40
'B17' No 2860 *Hull City* passes Staverton Road signalbox on
an up stopping train in the late 1930s.   *G. Coltas*

6 The Last Phase

The first move towards the introduction of larger engines on the GC was the installation of longer turntables at Marylebone and Leicester, referred to in the previous chapter. These were scheduled to come into use during the summer of 1938, and it is presumed that the plan was for the older Pacifics displaced on the GN Section by newly-built streamliners to be transferred to the GC. The last 'A4' was delivered in July, but at that time the new turntables were not quite ready; the one at Leicester Loco was tested on 16 August by No 4480 *Enterprise*, which came specially from Doncaster with Inspector Ted Slaughter on the footplate; Inspector Slaughter would know Leicester particularly well as he was a former GC man from Sheffield. Following this visit of No 4480 there were no further developments for a few weeks, probably because the turntable at Marylebone was not ready, and so it was not until late September that the first Pacific was transferred permanently to the GC.

There was a leisurely quality about the implementation of the new scheme, particularly as the first engine remained the only member of its class on the GC for over four months. This was despite the delivery of a number of new 'Green Arrows' to the GN Section, which ought in principle to have freed still more of the older engines, and the introduction of more intensive working there, a move which probably had the effect of reducing the number of engines required. In all probability the truth is that the GN Section sheds were reluctant to part with these dependable and extremely popular locomotives.

Before the arrival of the first Pacific in September a few isolated workings of these engines had been noted on the GC. With the introduction of the new overnight services to Newcastle, the working of which was shared by Gateshead Loco, Pacifics sometimes worked up to Leicester and may have filled in their stop-over time by working odd turns to Sheffield or Marylebone. The increasing weight of the 'Scotch Goods', which was worked nightly from York to Woodford by Doncaster engines, resulted in the occasional use of Pacifics, and members of the class were also seen on the 7.30am up express from Sheffield, this being another train which had recently become much heavier. None of these occurrences however involved engines actually based on the GC, and so the arrival of No 2558 *Tracery* at Gorton was something completely new.

The official date of its transfer was 19 September, but there are no reports of it at work until more than a week later. On Monday 27 September it took the 8.20am Marylebone express out of Manchester London Road, and worked it as far as Leicester. This was the outward leg of a Gorton diagram which had recently been revived after having lapsed about 10 years before; having turned at Leicester, the engine was scheduled to return as far as Sheffield on the 10am Marylebone-Bradford express, due out of Leicester at 12.6pm, and then to reach Manchester on an express from Cleethorpes which left Sheffield at 1.46pm. The diagram had been regularly worked by 'Footballers' up to this date, and one wonders what sort of attention this unaccustomed visitor attracted as it performed these tasks, the last a somewhat menial one for such a dignified monster. The casual observer may well have concluded that this was just another of the occasional Pacific workings already mentioned, but in fact the event was a milestone in GC history; it marked the beginning of a new phase, and the last under prewar conditions, in which both Pacifics and 'Green Arrows' were to claim an increasing share of the express passenger workings.

On the next day No 2558 worked the 8.20am turn again, and then on the Wednesday it was switched to a job that was afterwards to be much more closely associated with the class, the through working to London. The long-distance turns had been reduced from three to two following the reorganisation mentioned in the previous chapter, and whereas the working of the 2.20 up and 3.20 down afternoon expresses had been formerly shared between Gorton and Neasden they were now operated exclusively by men and engines from the northern end. The turns were covered by two engines and crews working opposite each other, with the usual overnight lodging at Neasden, and to cover the whole of a week's working it was necessary to diagram up and down through workings on Sundays as well as on the other days; the trains involved in this were the 5.35pm up from Manchester Central and the 5.30pm down from Marylebone. The Gorton men who started off their week's working on the Sunday did a total of four round trips, lodging at Neasden on Sunday, Tuesday, Thursday and Saturday. A curiosity of the up Sunday evening working was that instead of leaving Manchester with the 5.35pm the engine and crew worked to Sheffield with the 4.50pm stopping train from Manchester London Road and then waited there to take over the London train, which came in behind an engine of the Gorton No 2 Link. The purpose of this arrangement was to save light engine mileage between Gorton Loco and Manchester Central, the No 2 Link engine being already at Central after arriving there on a previous working; by the summer of 1938 the latter was usually a 'K3' 2-6-0. An entry in the *Railway Observer* of May 1939 gives an instance of this working, with an RCTS party reported as returning from Manchester on the 5.35pm, worked to Sheffield by an unidentified 'K3', and then forward by No 4478 *Hermit*, one of the Pacifics which followed No 2558 to the GC.

The appearance of No 2558 at Marylebone on 28 and 29 September evidently gave the first inkling of what was happening to observers in that part of the world, for when it repeated the diagram on the Friday and Saturday several interested spectators were on the scene, and the engine was photographed departing with the 3.20pm down. According to the *Railway Magazine* it took out a train of 10 vehicles, estimated at about 360 tons — not by any means a bad load for the GC in autumn. So ended what is believed to have been *Tracery's* first week of GC working.

The *Railway Magazine* report includes a somewhat vague reference to the fact that tests were being made with the Pacific, and in this connection it is interesting that the official records show No 2558 visiting Doncaster Plant between 13 and 19 September for a repair which included the fitting of a speed recorder described as being 'for the GC'. The date of its release from the works is also that of its transfer to Gorton, and perhaps the reason why there are no reports of it on main line turns in the succeeding week was because it was being run-in, although it is clear that the work of repair did not involve very much. The engine had been in the works for a general repair in the previous June, and may have had to go back in because a defect had developed.

As well as giving some significance to the remark in the *Railway Magazine*, the presence of the speed recorder also lends credence to a rumour current at the time that an Inspector had been seen on the footplate of No 2558. Probably his most important task would be to see how well the crew coped with the physically taxing job of covering the whole length of the difficult GC road with a Pacific, in view of the large firebox and unfamiliar controls.

On the Saturday that No 2558 performed its second trip with the 3.20 down, it acquired its first partner, and this somewhat surprisingly was not a sister Pacific but a 'Green Arrow', No 4798. The date of its official transfer to Gorton is 1 October and it is known to have gone into service working opposite No 2558, though precise dates have not been easy to come by. The arrival of a 'V2' rather conflicts with the usual view that the improvements on the GC were carried out in order to pave the way for displaced Pacifics, especially as more of the former were to arrive later, but possibly the explanation for the arrival of No 4798 at this stage is that it was sent for an extended trial prior to a decision about additional 'V2s' being used on the GC.

As was the case with No 2558, it must not be supposed that No 4798 was the first of the class to work on the Marylebone line. As early as the previous spring 'Green Arrows' were being used with some frequency on the overnight 'Scotch Goods', usually returning with the through Penzance-Aberdeen coaches on the 7.42pm departure from Banbury. On odd occasions they found their way to Marylebone when working this turn. The engines noted were usually from Doncaster, but York 'V2s' also appeared from time to time. NE Area 'V2s' were sometimes used on the Newcastle-Marylebone night passenger working.

Diagrammed on a regular basis for the same turns week in and week out. Nos 2558 and 4798 were of course 'common-user' engines, passing through the hands of different crews as the jobs rotated through the Top Link. In addition, they were also taken over by a completely separate crew each night they spent in London; as a result of the economy drive an arrangement was made whereby the engine arriving at Neasden Loco off the 2.20pm up

working was used on the 2.32am Newspaper train from Marylebone to Leicester. These changes brought to an end some long-established and much-cherished practices, notably the custom that senior drivers were allowed to retain their own engines, a system that had been adhered to closely at Gorton despite many difficulties. An equally significant change was the decision to diagram the Gorton engine for additional work during its overnight stay; as was pointed out in Chapter 4, the engines working on the long-distance turns were regarded as almost sacred, and never even in the most dire emergency was there any question of them being borrowed for other turns. The breaking of this unwritten rule was a very clear indication of the extent to which times had changed; nothing could have brought home more clearly to the Loco Running staff the urgency behind the economy programme.

Under this arrangement the engine was thus booked to do the 206-mile trip to London, spend about five hours at Neasden Loco for reconditioning and examining, do another 206 miles on the round trip to Leicester and back, spend a further six hours at Neasden and then make the long return journey to Manchester. The whole diagram involved working a total of 624 miles in not much over 24 hours, exclusive of light engine and empty stock working, with considerably less than 12 hours spent at the shed. All the duties were of an arduous nature except for the return working from Leicester, which was a fairly light stopping train due out at 6.21am.

In view of the prevailing prejudices, it is interesting to have some details of the men's reaction to the Pacifics and 'Green Arrows'. The presence of a trailing bogie under the cab eliminated much of the uncomfortable riding which was a source of so many complaints about the 'B17s' and 'K3s', and the roomy cab was generally more comfortable. The pull-out regulators were objected to because of stiffness, as they were when the first Pacifics came to Gorton soon after Grouping, and are said to have been a cause of slipping when starting off. For the fireman, the wide grate was the main bugbear, and there were reports of hands being burned during the process of filling up the back corners, as there had been at Sheffield when the GN Atlantics were first sent there. In general however the GC crews seem to have settled down well with the engines, and in part the reason for this may have been the fact that by 1938 a new generation of men were on the job who had not had the long years of experience with GC types on fast passenger work that undoubtedly created such a distrust of Doncaster engines. With the exception of Jack Glover and David Horne, the members of the Gorton Top Link were comparatively new to passenger work on the London line; these included George Bourne, Jack Garston and Tommy Evans, all of whom had been promoted into the link during 'B17' days. David Horne retired in January 1939, and after his place had been taken for a short time by a driver who did not settle to long-distance work, the vacancy was filled by Jim Fielding, a Gorton stalwart of many years' experience in the No 2 Link, always known as 'Hell-fire Jim'. Unhappily he collapsed and died on the footplate at Marylebone at the beginning of August, and for the last few weeks of regular through working to London his place was taken by Reuben Eastwood. At Neasden the senior drivers were George Parks, Ted Simpson, Jack Proctor and Jack Fisher, all having stepped into the shoes of the generation who had operated the 'D11s' and 'B3s' up to the mid-1930s. By this time of course they were no longer working through to Manchester as their predecessors had done.

Records of the first months of running by the big engines are surprisingly scarce after the initial publicity. No 2558 was noted on the up Sunday evening working of 2 October, and made its third successive return working on the 3.20 down of Monday; it is known to have made many trips to Marylebone between then and the end of the year, but few details have survived and it cannot be said for certain whether its employment on the turns was continuous or whether it was interrupted for any length of time. The earliest note of No 4798 is Wednesday 30 November, when it arrived right time at Manchester Central with the rather modest load of six vehicles.

Daily workings of the two engines in the Manchester district were interesting because they could be seen both in London Road and Central stations. On the up journey departure was from the former, but the return trip brought the engine via the Fallowfield line into Central. Arrival was at 7.45pm, and after being released from its train via the platform cross-over the engine coupled up tender-first to the empty stock and worked it to Gorton via the Fallowfield route and the Hyde Road curve; the coaches were then propelled into the carriage shed where they were prepared for the 8.20 outward working next morning. This empty stock working did not take place on Saturday evenings as the coaches were diagrammed for the 5.35pm express from Central; they were taken to the Cornbrook carriage shed by a pilot engine and the train engine ran light to Gorton. The journey tender first via the Hyde Road curve brought the engine into Gorton facing the right way for the next day's up journey and so the engine did not need to be turned for this.

In the event of the regular engines failing, the working was covered by 'Footballers', of which a number were at Gorton and Nos 2857/66 at Neasden. At both ends it was arranged that one of these engines should stand by at the time of departure of the long-distance engine.

Towards the end of January 1939 'V2' No 4798 went to Doncaster for repair, and 'B17s' were used to cover this gap in the ranks. The interlude was soon to be brought to an end by the arrival of a second Pacific, but is of some interest in affording the 'Footballers' their last regular opportunity of working the through turns. On 15 February the 3.20 down was noted behind No 2872 *West Ham United*, and this engine is likely to have put in a concentrated spell of long-distance duty during this period as it appears to have been one of Gorton's favourites. Its short reign came to an end on 25 February, when No 4474 *Victor Wild* reached Gorton and quickly took up its allotted share of the through working, being noted on the 3.20 on 1 March, less than a week later.

Further changes quickly followed. On Saturday 4 March No 4478 *Hermit* came to Gorton, a move which resulted in the transfer to the GE Section of one of the shed's best-loved 'Footballers', No 2862 *Manchester United*. The newcomer was soon noted working in tandem with No 2558, and this was the beginning of a partnership which lasted until May, apart from odd occasions when a 'B17' deputised because of failure. The following notes give some examples:

1939	Engine	Train
Wed 8 March	2558	3.20 down
Sat 11 March	4478	3.20 down
Tue 14 March	2558	3.20 down
Sat 18 March	2558	3.20 down
Thu 23 March	4478	3.20 down
Sat 25 March	4478	3.20 down
Wed 29 March	4478	3.20 down
Sat 1 April	4478	2.20 up
Sun 2 April	4478	5.30 down
Sat 8 April	4478	3.20 down
Sun 9 April	2558	5.30 down
Fri 21 April	4478	2.20 up
Sun 23 April	4478	5.35 up
Mon 24 April	4478	3.20 down
Fri 28 April	4478	3.20 down

The absence of No 4474 *Victor Wild* from the above list will be noted. After working the 3.20 down on 1 March as mentioned, it was next observed on 18 March arriving at Marylebone with the 10am up Bradford express. This was a Leicester working, and it is clear that within a few days of being sent to Gorton it was transferred to Leicester and took up regular work there. It worked a very full day beginning with the northbound morning 'Newspaper' train which it worked to Sheffield, and then returned as far as Leicester with the 7.30am Sheffield-Marylebone train; following a brief visit to shed it took the up Bradford express to London, due out at 12.47pm, and finally came back to Leicester on the 6.20pm down Bradford express. All the trains were fairly heavy, and the 6.20pm in particular had always ranked as one of Leicester's hardest jobs, while the greatly increased weight of the 7.30am ex-Sheffield has already been mentioned; the extra power of the Pacific was therefore well used on this diagram.

On 1 May Gorton acquired its third Pacific, No 4473 *Solario*. It was noted working the 2.20 up express on 19 May, and appears to have replaced No 2558 on the through workings for a time. With three of the class now on its strength, Gorton was in a position to diagram a Pacific for other turns besides the London jobs, and one of these was the 8.20 morning turn from Manchester London Road which was worked by No 2558 when it first arrived. Bringing the engine back to Gorton Loco in mid-afternoon, this diagram was usually coupled with an evening turn to Sheffield on the 6.31pm train from London Road, with a return from Sheffield at 8.31. The 6.31pm was made up of heavy express stock which would form the 7.30am Marylebone train the next morning.

On 18 May the second 'Green Arrow' arrived on the GC Section, and having only just been completed at Darlington claimed the distinction of being the first brand-new member of its class to be put into service on GC metals; this was No 4830, sent to Leicester in place of No 2856 *Leeds United*, which had been transferred to Cambridge the previous day. It is believed to have done some work on the overnight Marylebone-Newcastle trains, but also took a share in normal GC line workings. A contemporary issue of the *Railway Magazine* noted an unidentified Leicester 'Green Arrow' working into Marylebone with the 8.20am express from Manchester — this a Leicester working of long standing — while in addition No 4830 was timed by Sir James Colyer-Fergusson on the 6.20 down Bradford express, and was also photographed on this train. It may for a period have shared these workings on a turn-and-turn-about basis with Leicester's Pacific, No 4474.

The next round of changes took place at Neasden, when 'A1s' Nos 2546 *Donovan* and 2552 *Sansovino* were sent there in June. The earliest available record of their working is on Monday 10 July, when No 2552 was noted on the heavy 10.5pm Mail out of Marylebone; it was seen on this train several times subsequently. The diagram involved working as far as Leicester and returning with the up Mail from Manchester. Both Mail trains often loaded to 11 or 12 vehicles and so the additional capacity of the Pacifics was put to very good use; prior to the arrival of the engines at Neasden the down Mail was often double-headed.

Another working for the Neasden Pacifics was the 10am down Bradford express, a long-standing Neasden turn on which the engines had always worked as far as Leicester; however the return working was now altered, so that instead of coming back with a Leicester-Marylebone stopping train as Neasden engines had done in the past, the Pacific returned on the up Bradford express due out of Leicester at 12.47pm. This change was no doubt made in order to utilise the Pacific's capacity more fully. Neasden men also used Pacifics on the 2.32am Newspaper turn, but as described earlier, the engines were from Gorton; this arrangement had given the main line men valuable experience of Pacifics before the shed acquired its own. As at Gorton, the large engines were operated on a common-user basis, being diagrammed for specific turns instead of following the drivers through the link.

The arrival of two more brand-new 'Green Arrows' at Gorton during June is a clear indication that the class had won their spurs on the GC Section, as they had elsewhere, and suggests that a policy of wholesale re-equipment was now being carried out. The new arrivals, Nos 4832/3, were used on the 8.20am diagram described earlier, and also worked regularly over the Cheshire Lines Railway, taking the Liverpool portion of the overnight down Mail forward from Godley to Liverpool Central via Stockport Tiviot Dale and returning with the 8.30am Liverpool-Hull train. Apparently there was very little room to spare on the turntable at Brunswick Loco when a 'Green Arrow' was being turned, and an accident occurred when a man was crushed between the tender back and an adjacent wall.

It is interesting that the Gorton 'Green Arrows' were apparently not used on the through workings. On two successive Saturdays, 3 and 10 June, No 2866 *Nottingham Forest* of Neasden was noted leaving London Road with the 2.20 up, evidently having been substituted for a Pacific which had failed in London, where it was still the regular stand-by, and one wonders whether the Gorton men might not have preferred to take one of the new 2-6-2s and have the 'B17' sent back to London by some other means. Possibly the reluctance to use the 'Green Arrows' arose simply from a desire to restrict the through workings to named engines. The 2.20 up and 3.20 down were still very much the crack trains of the GC, and had always been worked by named engines up to the appearance of No 4798 late in 1938. This could also be the reason for the use of *Nottingham Forest* as a stand-by.

Apart from the odd appearances of the latter, Nos 4473 and 4478 seem to have had a spell of regular partnership on the London turns lasting several weeks, and the old favourite No 2558 *Tracery* was not noted until Wednesday 19 July, when it worked the 2.20 up, returning the following day on the down working. It had previously been noted on 11 May in charge of the down train, although with gaps in the records it cannot be said with certainty that it never appeared on the turns between then and 19 July.

By August a position had been reached whereby almost all of the principal GC main line express passenger trains were being monopolised by Pacifics and 'Green Arrows'. The list of trains that were more or less regularly worked by them reads as follows:

2.32pm down Newspaper	(Neasden and Leicester sheds)
10am down Bradford	(Neasden and Gorton)
3.20pm down Manchester	(Gorton)
6.20pm down Bradford	(Leicester engine as far as Leicester)
10.5pm down Mail	(Neasden engine to Leicester)
7.30am ex-Sheffield	(Leicester engine as far as Leicester)
8.20am ex-Manchester	(Gorton and Leicester)
10am ex-Bradford	(Neasden engine forward from Leicester)
2.20pm ex-Manchester	(Gorton)
10.30pm up Mail	(Neasden engine forward from Leicester)

In addition, Doncaster was using 'Green Arrows' on the northbound 'Penzance-Aberdeen'.

Of the three trains not included in this list, the 8.45am down and 3.50pm up were worked by Leicester, and large engines may well have been introduced on them during August as Leicester received No 2562 *Isinglass* and 'V2' No 4845 in that month. The third train, the 12.15pm down, was a Gorton job north of Leicester, and during August the shed increased its allocation of Pacifics to four with the arrival of No 2554 *Woolwinder*, so that either a Pacific or 'Green Arrow' is likely to have been diagrammed for this job from then on. The only shed which remained unaffected by the invasion was Sheffield, and this was a tribute to the excellence of the GN Atlantics, which continued to operate the Hull-Liverpool trains and several turns to Leicester with conspicuous success.

Apart from a stud of 10 based at Leicester, mainly for use on the north-to-west trains, the Class B17 'Footballers' had by now been almost eliminated from the GC. Gorton's allocation had been reduced to two, Nos 2864 *Liverpool* and 2869 *Barnsley*, and at Neasden only No 2866 survived. Late in August this engine was transferred to Gorton to take the place of No 2864, which had gone in for repair, and it is to be presumed that from then onwards Neasden arranged for one of its Pacifics to cover the 3.20 down working. Woodford had acquired three 'B17s' in the spring of 1937, as mentioned in the previous chapter, for use on the north-to-west trains, and in July 1939 all were transferred to Sheffield; this move did not herald any replacement of the firmly-established GN Atlantics, but took place because the Swindon working was about to be recommenced.

The 'B17' decline continued into September, with Nos 2848/65/68 leaving Leicester for the GE Section. Of these, No 2865 had not worked from Leicester Loco since early July, having been under repair at Gorton. Nos 2849 and 2851, both of Leicester, were also under repair early in September, as was Sheffield's newly-acquired No 2855

and both the Gorton 'Footballers'. There were thus only about half a dozen of the class active on the GC at this period, a situation very greatly changed from that of only 12 months before. It seems likely that the process of replacement by larger engines might have continued had not the outbreak of war put a different complexion on matters.

The wholesale withdrawal of GC Section express passenger services soon after the start of the war marks the end of this story. During the early war years further Pacifics were drafted in, and dominated the scene for some time, but the service had by this time been so drastically curtailed as to be unrecognisable, and no true comparison with the prewar situation is possible. But there can be no doubt that the changes of 1938-9 were in reality the most significant of all those which took place between the wars, and had there been no war in 1939 the types which were by that time working on the GC Section would never have been displaced.

41

No 2558 *Tracery*, first Pacific to work regularly on the GC, prepares to depart from Platform 4 at Marylebone with the 'Sam Fay' down on 1 October 1938. This was the end of its first week of normal work on the GC. *B. K. Cooper*

42
No 4833 one of Gorton's 'Green Arrows', is on the 12.15pm
Marylebone-Manchester express at Bagthorpe Junction on
19 August 1939.
T. G. Hepburn/Rail Archive Stephenson

43
'V2' No 4830 of Leicester approaches Staverton Road
signalbox on a down stopping train in 1939.   *G. Coltas*

44
Gorton's Jack Glover leans confidently out of the cab of
No 2558 *Tracery* as he takes the 2.20pm up express out of
Nottingham Victoria, on 8 May 1939.
T. G. Hepburn/Rail Archive Stephenson

45
One of the last Pacifics allocated to Gorton before the start
of war, No 2554 *Woolwinder* enters Nottingham Victoria
with the 2.20 up express on 23 August 1939.
T. G. Hepburn/Rail Archive Stephenson

46

46
No 4831 *Durham School* of Gateshead shed makes a rare
appearance at Nottingham Victoria with a return
Scarborough-Leicester train on 1 July 1939; this was a
regular summer season working.
T. G. Hepburn/Rail Archive Stephenson

47
The 'Sam Fay' down leaves Nottingham Victoria behind
No 4478 *Hermit* on 17 August 1939.
T. G. Hepburn/Rail Archive Stephenson

48
Gorton's second 'Green Arrow', No 4828, is at the up end of
Godley Station on 1 June 1939, having arrived to work the
Manchester London Road portion of the afternoon Hull-
Liverpool express detached at Godley. *A. Appleton*

47

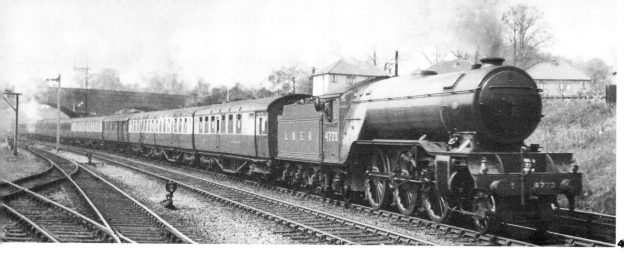

49
Sunderland supporters travel to Wembley behind York's
No 4773, seen here passing Sudbury Hill. It is Cup Final day
1937, and their team was to defeat Preston North End.
C. R. L. Coles

50
Gorton's No 4478 *Hermit* passes Northwood with the 'Sam
Fay' down in the summer of 1939.   *C. R. L. Coles*

51
A Leicester 'Green Arrow', No 4830, leaves Nottingham
Victoria with the 12.15pm Manchester-Marylebone express
on Sunday 18 June 1939.
T. G. Hepburn/Rail Archive Stephenson

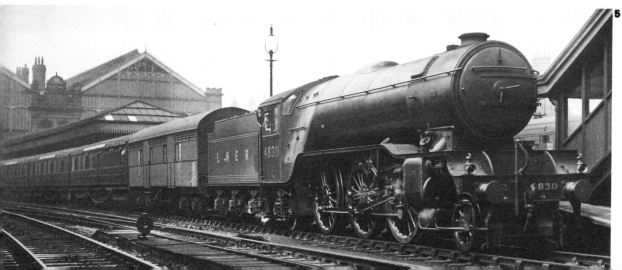

7 'Promptitude'

'Promptitude' was the nickname given to the 4.55pm express out of Marylebone, which during the 1930s was the fastest GC train between the capital and Manchester; though its career was not a very long one, it held the Blue Riband for speed on the GC. First introduced as a Marylebone-Sheffield train in 1929, it was extended to Manchester the following year, and thus ranks as the most notable addition to the GC fast passenger services in the interwar years. Alas however, the speedy schedule failed to attract the anticipated business, and in late 1938 the flier suffered the indignity of being cut back once again to Sheffield. Its career as a Manchester express therefore belongs entirely to the vintage years when standards of locomotive and track maintenance were high enough to permit speeds in the 90s, and we may be sure that in order to keep to its typically tight GC schedule the 4.55 would often have touched 90mph on favourable stretches.

Following the discontinuance of the notably unsuccessful experiment with the Pullman service between Manchester and Kings Cross in 1925, the GC express passenger service reverted to what was in effect its final pre-Grouping state, and was to stay like that for some time. In view of the developments that were taking place on the East Coast main line it seems surprising that there should have been such stagnation on the GC, even allowing for the much greater importance of the Kings Cross route, and it is tempting to suggest that after burning their fingers with the Pullman service the management were loth to tamper further with the Marylebone trains. However the nettle was eventually grasped in July 1929, when a whole series of adjustments to the passenger services were brought into effect, the principal one being the introduction of the new Marylebone-Sheffield train. These constituted the most important alterations to the GC passenger timetables ever made between the Grouping and the war, and are worth looking at in some detail.

The new 4.55pm express replaced a previous 4.55 which had been a stopping train from Marylebone to Woodford via High Wycombe; this was retimed to leave five minutes earlier, was speeded up, and now terminated at Brackley instead of Woodford. To cater for Woodford passengers a stop was inserted into the schedule of the 5pm Marylebone-Mansfield express, a move which left them considerably better off as they could now reach Woodford 40 minutes earlier than by the original train. Several other additional stops were incorporated into the schedule of the 5pm express, and this came down considerably in prestige as a result, losing its restaurant car facilities and being cut back to Nottingham. The restaurant car crew transferred to the new 4.55, which thus to some extent took the place of the former Marylebone-Mansfield express, even to the point of making connection with a Nottingham-Mansfield train which reached the latter at almost the same time as the 5pm had done previously.

In the opposite direction a new 7.30pm through train from Sheffield to Marylebone was put on to replace the previous 7.30 which had connected with the up morning Mansfield express to Nottingham; this new up train became a morning counterpart of the 4.55 as it formed the return working of the coaching stock. The coaches thus remained overnight in Sheffield, where they were cleaned and examined in the carriage shed at Bernard Road, a short distance east of Sheffield Victoria on the down side of the main line. In the time between their arrival in Marylebone at 10.40am and subsequent departure at 4.55 in the evening they were stored in the carriage sidings just outside the terminus.

Why the departure time of 4.55 should have been chosen is not known. In the days before World War 1 there had been a train out of Marylebone at 4.35, but it took over four hours to reach Sheffield and was not in any way comparable with the 1929 train. It is interesting that the margin of time separating the 4.55 from the previous down express, the 3.20pm 'Sam Fay Down' was 1hr 35min, exactly the same as that between the 2.15pm and 3.50 up expresses from Manchester, though whether this was chance or design cannot be said.

The extent to which the 4.55 stood supreme in GC speed can be seen by comparing it with the 3.20pm down, descendant of Sir Sam Fay's 'Sheffield Special' and formerly pre-eminent among trains out of Marylebone. The new express was one minute quicker to Leicester, and when extended to Manchester in 1930 was timed to get there all of 25 minutes earlier, although admittedly by the much more direct route to London Road, its rival having to negotiate the rather circuitous route through the south Manchester suburbs to reach Central station. It could therefore claim to be easily the quickest south-to-north train on GC metals.

The image of the 4.55 received a further boost from the provision of new LNER-built stock complete with restaurant car and all-electric kitchen as recently pioneered on the 'Flying Scotsman'. The gleaming coaches complete with varnished teak panelling and white roofs were maintained internally and externally in superb condition by the cleaning staff at Sheffield. The GC Section carriage stock diagrams of July 1929 show that as first introduced the 4.55 was made up to the somewhat modest complement of five coaches, listed as an open third, restaurant first, corridor composite and the usual brake third at each end. Seating was given as 39 first class passengers and 144 third, although from what is known of the train it is doubtful if even these comparatively few places were ever completely filled in normal service.

New LNER stock was provided for the other principal GC expresses at the same time, and the appearance of these vehicles was a visible sign that the LNER was beginning to make its influence felt outside the confines of the East Coast main line. GC kitchen and restaurant car staff had gained experience of working with the new type of stock after a set of Gresley-type coaches had been sent on trial about 1927.

In common with most GC expresses the new train was diagrammed for an engine-change at Leicester, the traditional 'half-way house' of the GC. The Neasden engine and men formerly diagrammed to work the 5pm Marylebone-Mansfield train as far as Leicester now transferred to the new flier, returning from Leicester on the same home working as previously. The train was taken over at Leicester by a fresh engine coming off Leicester Loco, and formed a distinguished new working for the men of Leicester, whose strategic position midway along the north-south route had always ensured them a good share of the express passenger workings. Arrival in Sheffield was at 8.2pm, and the Leicester engine then ran light to Rotherham to return home on the York-Bristol Mail.

Such was 'Promptitude' during its first few months of existence. The decision to extend it to Manchester on 1 January 1930, after only six months of operation as a London-Sheffield train was probably an attempt to generate better custom following a disappointing initial response. The move was very unfortunately timed however, as it coincided almost exactly with the very worst of the depression. During the next two years LNER revenues from all sources were to fall to not much more than half of what they had been in 1929, and with the north-west being particularly badly affected by the severe decline in the cotton trade it is remarkable that the train managed to survive. But survive it did and although the 4.55 could certainly never claim to have been anywhere near the best-patronised express on the GC it did succeed in staying the course almost through to the outbreak of the war.

However doubtful the train's future may have seemed at the time, the new development was full of interest from a purely railway point of view. A non-stop run of 59min between Sheffield and Manchester — a record-breaking schedule — was something to make the railway fraternity sit up and take notice, and it was not long before this section of the run began to attract the attention of train-timers, including the now very well-known Cecil J. Allen; his account will be mentioned in detail later. Completing the London-to-Manchester journey in a total of 4hr 10min, the newly extended 4.55 was in a class of its own, but even so it is worth noting that the time compared poorly with the best LMS trains over the LNW line from Euston; because of the much more direct route they were able to reach London Road comfortably in 3¾hr. Even the rather more leisurely Midland Division could still show a slightly better time with the 12.25pm from St Pancras, which got into Manchester in just under four hours.

For the new run to Manchester a change of engines was made at Sheffield, and 'Promptitude' thus became one of the very few GC expresses to be hauled by three separate engines on the run between London and the north. Four minutes were allowed for the change, as at Leicester, and the train's standard of timekeeping indicates that, as ever, both these changes were carried

out with the usual GC smartness and precision. On its final stage the 4.55 was taken forward by a Gorton engine and men, working a somewhat curious diagram which involved nothing more than an out-and-back trip between Manchester and Sheffield, the outward working being on a stopping train. The engine was thus quite fresh and would have had little difficulty in keeping the 59-minute schedule, especially if it happened to be a 'Director', as was often the case. Whilst waiting at Sheffield Victoria the Gorton engine also covered for the 3.20pm down express, which arrived at 6.26pm with the engine having come through from London. Despite this dual purpose the Gorton diagram was obviously a rather wasteful one, but it was entirely characteristic of the GC under Maclure's viziership that Gorton Loco should have some hand in the working of this crack train.

Travellers on the new express thus had the privilege of riding behind some of the best engines on the GC system, with the three leading passenger sheds all being involved. With an ample fleet of 'Directors' on its strength, Neasden usually turned out an engine of this type for the London-Leicester stage of the journey, although sometimes one of the Caprotti-fitted 'Lord Faringdons' might be found at the head of the train. At Leicester it was the turn of the faithful 'C4' Atlantics which did so much sterling work there during the inter-war years; they worked the train with unvarying regularity until displaced by 'B17s' some years later. Gorton usually provided a Director, setting the pattern by turning out No 5438 Worsley-Taylor on the inaugural run of 1 January; this engine was one of Gorton's best 'D10s'.

Mr C. J. Allen's article about the Sheffield-Manchester portion of the working has already been mentioned. In the Railway Magazine of July 1931 four logs are given, all showing clearly enough that the 59-minute schedule could be completed well inside time by the Gorton engines; all arrivals were early, and the quickest time of the four was actually put up by a mixed traffic engine with 5ft 7in driving wheels, 'B7' No 5072. On this trip, London Road was reached 5min ahead of schedule, and one has the impression that the crew were enjoying themselves. Work of this kind undoubtedly reflects much credit on both men and locomotives, but it is clear that the easy nature of the diagram contributed a good deal towards the results, a point not brought out by Mr Allen. The uphill stretch from Sheffield to Dunford Bridge was of course much more severe than anything encountered to the south, but the distance of 41.3 miles hardly compares, for example with the 103 miles which the Neasden engines had to cover on the working to Leicester.

The retimetabling of the 4.55 brought about considerable alteration to the GC Section carriage workings. Because of its late-evening arrival in Manchester London Road, the stock of the 4.55 could no longer form the morning express from Sheffield as there was no convenient Manchester-Sheffield train by which it could be conveyed there. It was now re-diagrammed to go to the Gorton carriage sheds, remaining there overnight to form the 2.15pm up Marylebone express the next day; other arrangements were made for the 7.30am from Sheffield.

With this alteration, the coaches of 'Promptitude' and the 2.15 up express were different from other main-line sets in being diagrammed for a single through trip each day instead of working out-and-home; this meant that two sets of stock were required to operate the two trains, working opposite each other on alternate days. To equalise the mileage with other sets, arrangements were made to switch the coaches to another diagram at weekends, so that the single-trip working was performed by different sets of stock on different weeks.

The somewhat cumbersome system whereby the 4.55 was worked by three separate engines did not survive very long once Maclure had retired in March 1931. The very incomplete records of 4.55 workings which have survived show that Gorton were still in charge of the Sheffield-Manchester part of the run 12 months after Maclure's departure from the scene, when No 5511 *Marne* worked the turn on 5 March 1932 with Jack Hopley at the regulator, but by the following autumn the train was arriving in Manchester behind Leicester engines; instead of coming off at Sheffield as formerly, these were now diagrammed to continue through to Manchester London Road, and it was in this form that 'Pomptitude' was to become so familiar to observers at the northern end of the GC during the 1930s. The exact date of the change has not been established, but in May 1932 there came a major alteration in the schedule of the 4.55 when a full five minutes were lopped off the Sheffield-Manchester time, and it is believed that the introduction of this very fast run coincided with the change in diagramming.

The speeding-up of the schedule, giving an arrival in Manchester at 9pm instead of 9.5 and putting the Sheffield-Manchester timing almost on a par with the electrification schedule of BR days, was part of the LNER programme of accelerations which in the past have received considerable publicity in respect of the East Coast main line, but of which little has so far been heard on the GC. The decision to improve timings at this stage probably sprang from a desire to stimulate traffic following the drastic fall in receipts caused by the depression, which at this date still held the country in its grip. The acceleration of the 4.55 was undoubtedly a considerable act of faith in view of the still unhappy state of things in 'Cottonopolis', as Manchester has sometimes been called, and in retrospect the fact that the 4.55 continued to run as long as it did seems more of a tribute to the company's perseverance than to its far-sightedness.

The newly extended Leicester diagram was notable in providing a particularly arduous outward working for the veteran Atlantic, which was now scheduled to go over 40 miles further than before and to climb Woodhead into the bargain, all in a total time of only 2hr 13min from the start. After arrival in Manchester the engine was diagrammed to back out with the stock, assisting the pilot engine out to the carriage sheds, and to turn at Gorton Loco; this left a few moments for the usual examination and then the engine was on its way back to London Road again for the homeward journey on the 10.30pm up Mail. For the local observers, the regular appearance of Leicester Atlantics was a source of great interest, as apart from periodic

visits to Gorton Works the 'C4s' were not at that period particularly common in their 'Mother City'; 'Promptitude' afforded an excellent opportunity of seeing one in the very pink of condition, although of course it was only at the height of midsummer that the spectacle could be savoured in daylight. The recollections of observers make it clear that the formidable climb from Sheffield to Dunford in no way handicapped these remarkable machines, and it has been told on a number of occasions how the clock of Manchester Town Hall was striking nine as the gleaming Atlantic drew gently up to the buffer-stops, thus amply justifying the train's proud nickname.

The Leicester Atlantics had a long spell on the northern half of the 4.55, and their regularity on the turn was typical of the consistency with which they performed so much of the work at Leicester Loco. Although the normal load of six coaches was not a heavy one, it should be borne in mind that by the time these engines began to work the turn they were approaching 30 years old. Nothing could indicate more clearly the virtues of Gorton methods of design, which laid great stress on solidity and durability. An instance of the great affection felt for the engines is to be seen in a recollection of Mr P. H. V. Banyard, who spent a lifetime at Leicester Loco and attained the rank of Inspector. He recalled an occasion in 1935 when he was firing for Driver Abraham Bennett on No 6090; with them on the footplate was Inspector Tommy Adams of Gorton, a well-known figure on the GC, and the engine had just begun the climb to Dunford with a load of 10 bogies. As they climbed steadily, the Inspector remarked 'The old lass is talking to us now'.

However it must be recorded that the crew would not have felt so happy about things on 14 February 1936, when one of the Atlantics dropped its motion on to the track about two miles inside Woodhead tunnel, so that engine and train became stranded inside and had to remain there until pulled out by another engine sent in specially. The identity of the train engine is not known, but this was one occasion when the 4.55 failed to live up to its reputation.

By the time this incident occurred time was fast running out for these beautiful veterans. The arrival of the 'Footballers' at Leicester has already been described in Chapter 6, and not surprisingly the 4.55 turn was one of the first on which they replaced the Atlantics. It is probable that the very first 'Footballer' to visit Manchester came in on this working, although no details of that occurrence have been traced. The earliest date on which one of the class is known to have headed the 9pm arrival into London Road is Monday 6 April, when No 2849 *Sheffield United* made an appearance. The engine had been at Leicester for a little over a week, having arrived on 26 March. It was used again on the following day, and then on the Wednesday it was the turn of another very recent arrival at Leicester Loco, No 2852 *Darlington*. At this stage there were only six 'Footballers' at Leicester altogether, and their appearances on the 4.55 show how important the working was considered to be. On the following Tuesday, 14 April, 'C4' No 6087 came to Manchester, a reminder that in the early period of

'Footballer' working the Atlantics were used as stand-by engines. They were however used only on isolated occasions, as the appearance of No 2850 *Grimsby Town* on the following day clearly indicates.

The 'Footballers' attracted considerable attention in Manchester, and the novelty of their names was much commented on. Despite the attractive splash of colour below the nameplate there seems to have been a feeling that in their relentless search for publicity the LNER had on this occasion overstepped the bounds of good taste; this is a curiously similar reaction to that expressed in certain quarters when the first streamliners appeared, and in both instances the criticism seems to have been only an initial response, little more being heard of it as people got used to the engines. Whatever one's feelings about the football club names, the sight of a brand-new 'Footballer' climbing to Dunford at the head of 'Promptitude' must have been something to remember.

It is interesting that in spite of the large number of these engines sent to the GC, as described in Chapter 5, they made comparatively little impact on the London-Leicester section of the 4.55 working. Neasden never had more than three of the class on its strength at any time, and by about 1937 and 4.55 was probably the only Marylebone-Manchester express which could still be observed with a Gorton-designed engine at the head. Even as late as June 1939 one of the poppet-valve 'Lord Faringdons', No 6166 *Earl Haig*, was noted on the working, and as by this time there was only one 'Footballer' at Neasden it is likely that either engines of the 'Lord Faringdon' class or else 'Directors' would have been regularly in charge of the 4.55.

In the *Railway Magazine* of July 1939 Mr C. J. Allen published details of four runs between Sheffield and Manchester which probably represent the most comprehensive coverage of 'B17' performance on the 4.55 turn. The engines concerned were No 2848 *Arsenal*, No 2852 *Darlington* and No 2853 *Huddersfield Town* twice; in all cases the engines are shown coping well with the train, although in three out of the four trips the load was the usual fairly light one — five, six and seven vehicles. Only in the run with No 2848 was there a substantial train of 10 bogies, and with such a load the crew did extremely well to lose no more than a fraction of a minute into Manchester. Such a task was clearly close to the upper limit of 'B17' haulage capacity, and it is interesting that a very experienced observer of GC affairs, the late F. H. Gillford, expressed the view that the class were not capable of handling trains of more than 10 vehicles north of Nottingham.

This performance of No 2848 also gives an insight into the capabilities of 'B17' engines on the whole range of GC

Section workings. It has been pointed out that the drawbar-horsepower exerted was only 1,100, as compared with a figure of 1,400 attained by No 2861 *Sheffield Wednesday* when on test during 1936, and that the effort of No 2848 was therefore somewhat below what could be achieved by a 'B17' in favourable conditions. Such an argument sounds very convincing, but it is certain that the results achieved by No 2861 would never have been possible under normal day-to-day conditions. Perhaps the most important point is that the horsepower figure of 1,400 was sustained for only five miles, which is barely a quarter of the distance between Sheffield Victoria and Dunford Bridge. Even if this high horsepower had been achieved by No 2848, or something approaching it, there is the relative difficulty of the turn to be considered. Despite the faster time between Sheffield and Manchester, the 4.55 working was actually easier than the 3.20, for two reasons. The absence of a stop at Penistone eliminated the very awkward restart on the steepest part of the gradient, marked at 1 in 100; and the engine was of course working only from Leicester instead of all the way

No 6166 *Earl Haig* is on Neasden Loco turntable in the early 1930s. This engine sometimes worked Neasden's portion of 'Promptitude'. *Photomatic*

from Marylebone. It ought also to be pointed out that the trip with No 2848 took place during the summer; the Woodhead line could be a very different place in the middle of winter, with both wind and weather adding considerably to the engine's task. To achieve a good standard of punctuality over the Woodhead line, the 'B17s' really needed to be limited to nine vehicles, and this was clearly not enough by the late 1930s.

It is sad to have to record that by the time the 4.55 logs appeared in print, 'Promptitude' had been cut back to terminate at Sheffield. This occurred in December 1938, and the decision was taken because of a very sharp recession in traffics which the country's railways experienced during that year. It is in any case doubtful whether the train ever loaded heavily apart from at the height of the holiday season, and according to observers it seldom exceeded seven vehicles. Therefore when a particularly noticeable drop in business became apparent, as it did during 1938, the 4.55 was one of the first trains to be reviewed. The fact that it was allowed to continue running as far as Sheffield indicates that on that section of the

route it was fairly well able to hold its own with the competing Midland line of the LMS, no doubt on account of the more direct route. So far as the Manchester traffic was concerned however, it was clearly unable to overcome the handicap of considerably greater distance.

The train was thus back to its 1929 condition, but did not have much longer to go. The outbreak of war in September 1939 saw an early rationalisation of the GC express passenger services which brought about the disappearance of a number of trains, including the 4.55. Thus did it pass into history, for although a number of the expresses were restored after the war, 'Promptitude' was not among them.

Though strictly a creation of the LNER, it embodied much that was typical of the GC, and the speed and punctuality of its operation are particularly characteristic of the 1930s. Nothing like it was ever to be seen again, and even the electrification of the Sheffield-Manchester section in the 1950s did not enable British Railways to offer comparable times between Marylebone and Manchester.

52

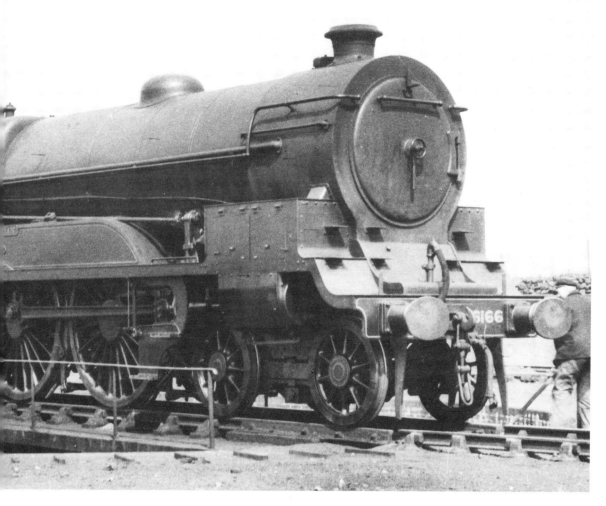

53

53
A winter evening scene at Marylebone. Leicester's No 2851 *Derby County* prepares to depart from Platform 4 with what is probably the 6.20 Bradford train. The date is 1937. *E. E. Smith*

54
No 5438 *Worsley-Taylor* is on a down express just north of Rickmansworth in the early 1930s. One of the Gorton's best 'D10s', this engine was chosen to work the first trip of 'Promptitude' from Sheffield to Manchester on 1 January 1930. *LNER Official Photo*

54

8 London Suburban

For obvious reasons, suburban work seldom attracts the attention enjoyed by express passenger trains. Yet from an operating point of view it offers features of very great interest, especially when such things as rush-hour services, or special traffic in connection with particular events are concerned. Suburban train services were to be found at both the northern and southern ends of the GC system, with the latter being considerably more modern and in some respects unique.

Though it could never claim to compete with the Liverpool Street and Kings Cross suburban services in terms of density, the Marylebone service was in a different category when it came to comfort, and the provision of larger engines from shortly before World War 1 had made it in many ways the showpiece of the old GCR system. From the turn of the century a new and rather select group of outer suburbs was growing up in the districts served by the GC network; the company did its best to cater for the new demand, and of course its efforts helped to attract more people to the area.

Basically the Marylebone suburban trains served two routes, both of approximately equal importance, and both of them lines worked jointly with other companies. The line to Aylesbury and Quainton Road, which included the Chesham branch and a service to Verney Junction, was held in a joint lease with the Metropolitan Railway, and was the Great Central's original means of entry into London. The other route had come into operation a few years after the opening of the London line and was jointly leased with the Great Western; it offered both companies an alternative route to the capital and at the same time tapped a valuable reservoir of suburban traffic, particularly in the vicinity of High Wycombe and Princes Risborough. During LNER days these two routes were served by a smartly-operated and in many ways typically Great Central suburban service which altered very little until after World War 2.

For Loco Running purposes the whole area was embraced in the lengthy tentacles of the Neasden Locomotive District, which extended as far north as the shed at Woodford, almost 70 miles away. It included a sub-shed at Aylesbury and a small one-road establishment adjacent to Marylebone Road Goods Depot, but the latter appears to have fallen into disuse at a very early stage and did not operate during LNER days.

The original motive power for the suburban trains were the 4-4-2 tanks later designated Classes C13 and C14 by the LNER. Before World War 1 they had been diagrammed so that the latter were used principally on the GW Joint Line whereas the 'C13s', which were the earlier series, found employment on the Metropolitan line. However the rapid development of the new suburbs already mentioned soon led to heavier trains, and a more powerful type of engine was needed. Such was the situation which led to the emergence in 1911 of the much larger 4-6-2 tanks later classed 'A5'; one of the most

successful locomotives ever to be designed by John G. Robinson, they were to dominate the Marylebone scene throughout LNER days.

Some measure of their success may be judged from the fact that even as the day of Grouping dawned, nearly 12 years after the first example had emerged from Gorton, engines of the class were still being built new for the Marylebone trains. All were based at Neasden, and by this date they had almost completely eliminated their smaller predecessors from the suburban services; the last survivor of these, 'C14' No 6125, departed for Langwith in May 1925. From then onwards the reign of the 'A5s' was to be completely uninterrupted apart from isolated appearances of Class N2 and N7 engines, which were usually sent to Neasden in exchange for 'A5s' transferred for varying periods of time to other parts of the LNER.

The year of Grouping was a time of great importance at Marylebone, quite apart from change of ownership. The finishing touches were just being put to the new Wembley Stadium, situated only a short distance from the terminus in the angle formed by the junction of the Metropolitan and GW Joint Lines, and here preparations were going ahead for the staging of the British Empire Exhibition in the following year; these included the construction of a loop line serving the Exhibition site, complete with a station to be used exclusively for the Exhibition and stadium. These events were not without effect on the railway services. In 1923, only four days after the huge stadium had been completed, the FA Cup Final was played there, an event which will long be remembered both in railway and sporting circles. It had been expected that the attendance at this game would be about the same as at the previous year's Final, when 53,000 spectators had been present, and it was therefore inevitable that neither railway nor stadium officials should be in any way prepared to handle the crowd of about 250,000 people which converged on Wembley that fateful afternoon. Occupation of the line into Marylebone was greatly increased by the arrival of 19 main line specials from the north, and in the opposite direction a steady stream of stadium specials had to be threaded through as larger and larger crowds of fans thronged the departure platforms. The whole service gradually ground to a halt, with trains standing nose-to-tail on both Wembley loop and main line, and the confusion was immediately made worse by the more impatient fans, who promptly descended on to the track and headed for the stadium on foot. This had the effect of paralysing the Metropolitan's electric service as the third rail had to be switched off for safety. An aerial photo taken shortly before the start of the game clearly shows people descending the cutting of the GW Joint Line at a point adjacent to the main grandstand and walking across the main line. By a miracle no one was killed or injured, but the nightmare for the staff can be better imagined than described. However the debacle furnished valuable lessons for the future which were learned very quickly by both railway and stadium management. One result was that admission to all future Wembley Cup Finals was to be by ticket only, instead of pay-at-the-door as had been the case in 1923.

A little less than 12 months later the stadium welcomed a large but on this occasion much more dignified and well-controlled crowd when on 23 April 1924 His Majesty King George V opened the British Empire Exhibition. This event proved to be the biggest attraction staged in Britain up to that time, drawing an estimated 15 million visitors before it closed towards the end of the year, and a further 7½ million when it reopened in 1925. Special trains from the Midlands and north arrived regularly at Marylebone, and a special exhibition service was run to the grounds, with trains going round the single-line loop in a clockwise direction. Extra engines were temporarily transferred to Neasden to cope with the additional demand, including several Class N7 0-6-2 tanks from the GE Section. Other unusual visitors were noted during this period, among them some small shunting engines such as 'J62' No 885 of Staveley Loco, and later a GER Tram engine, No 0125 from Wisbech. No 0129 of this type was also noted at Neasden in 1925, and towards the end of the year a NE Area engine, 'Y7' No 986, was observed; the last-mentioned was seen again as late as April 1926. It is believed that this rather curious assortment of engines was sent to help with the movement of empty coaching stock during the Exhibition, and may also have shunted the locomotive exhibits which were on view there. The main burden of the exhibition service however fell on the faithful 'A5s', supported by a few of the Class L1 'Crabs'.

Coincident with the final closure of the Exhibition in 1925 came yet another important event, the opening of the Metropolitan and GC Joint branch to Watford. This was only 2½ miles long and its construction had been long delayed, first by the Great War and then by the upheaval of Grouping. In its final years the Great Central had been reluctant to go ahead with the project, as in the Board's opinion it held out little prospect of a satisfactory financial return now that the company was to become part of the LNER. When eventually the work of construction was begun, engineering difficulties were encountered which considerably delayed its completion. The official opening was finally scheduled for 2 November 1925, and two days before this a special train hauled by a Metropolitan electric locomotive conveyed a party of officials over the branch, the GC interest being represented by the presence of Lord Faringdon and W. G. P. Maclure.

A very lavish passenger service was offered on this branch, with a total of 140 trains operating daily between Watford and London, destinations including Baker Street, Liverpool Street and Marylebone. Neasden Loco had the responsibility of providing about half the engines, the rest being from the Metropolitan. It seems likely that the last batch of 'A5' engines, built in the first half of 1923, were originally intended for this role, but when the branch finally opened the choice fell on the Class N7 tanks which had originally been imported for the Exhibition service.

These engines were soon found to have insufficient coal and water capacity to work the service satisfactorily and were superseded by the trusty 'A5s'. In the event the whole exercise proved to be very shortlived as far as the GC was concerned; coal shortages during the 1926 strike caused Neasden to suspend its share of the working, and an official announcement in the supplement to the LNER public timetables broke the news that from 1 January 1927 the company's service to Watford would be withdrawn. By this time the GE Section engines had been repatriated to East Anglia, and the branch operated henceforth as an all-electric line under Metropolitan auspices. It had in any case become apparent that the original service was considerably in excess of demand when a brief attempt to resuscitate the GC workings just before the end of 1926 indicated that the LNER trains were poorly patronised.

The serious interruption to the Watford service because of difficulties arising from the coal strike is a reminder of the fact that because of its great distance from the nearest centres of coal production Neasden Loco was particularly vulnerable to any form of interference with these vital supplies. The first taste of this had been experienced in late GCR days when the miners' strike of 1921 brought all production to a halt for a period of three months, compelling the railways to rely entirely on such stocks as were to hand. The Great Central found a partial solution in the conversion of several engines to oil-burning, and 10 of Neasden's 'A5s' were given an apparatus of this kind patented under the name of the 'Unolco' system. It is believed that when this was removed at the end of the strike, the management wisely decided to keep the equipment handy in the event of another bout of industrial unrest, and this prudent action was to be fully justified in 1926 when the second serious coal stoppage occurred. The oil-burning apparatus was brought into use again on six of the 'A5' engines, and at least four of these conversions were actually carried out at Neasden Loco. Coal production was resumed at the end of the year, and in April 1927 the last 'A5' was converted back to coal-firing.

An analysis of the Marylebone services as they stood in September 1928 shows that by this time a majority of the suburban trains were operating on the GW Joint Line. On weekdays 19 trains departed from Marylebone for destinations on the Metropolitan line, compared with 32 on the other route, and a similar proportion ran in the opposite direction. The presence of competing Metropolitan trains on the former line was the main reason for this difference.

The town which enjoyed easily the best service of the whole network was High Wycombe, with 16 arrivals and 15 departures every day except Saturdays and Sundays. In the down direction this service began with a 5.15am departure from Marylebone, and the last train of the day left at the very late hour of 11.50pm, with the empty stock returning to Marylebone after arrival. The first up train left at 6.33, and the last at 10.23pm. With a journey time varying from 42min to 1hr for the distance of over 27 miles, this was clearly a very attractive and competitive service.

Most other trains on the GW Joint Line terminated at points nearer to London, usually Ruislip or Denham, but there was one train in each direction serving Princes Risborough, and an even greater distance was covered by the 6.10am departure from Marylebone, which went right out to Wotton, beyond the divergence with the GWR line at Ashendon Junction; this train was due back in Marylebone at 9.55am, having left Wotton at 8.15. The longest distance of all was covered by the two down Brackley trains, the morning one going via the Metropolitan and its afternoon counterpart by the GW Joint. There were no corresponding up trains.

On the Metropolitan line the majority of trains served Aylesbury, and other destinations included Amersham, Chesham and Great Missenden, all three adjacent to each other.

Peak period services at Marylebone reveal the very light nature of the suburban traffic compared with that of its rivals Liverpool Street and Kings Cross. The morning rush-hour, if that is the correct term for it, began with the arrival at 7.35 of the 6.33 train from High Wycombe. Between then and 9 o'clock a further nine trains arrived at intervals varying from 4min to 13min. The last arrival was the 8.18 from High Wycombe, covering the journey in 42min with stops at Beaconsfield and Gerrards Cross, and a good example of the kind of smart working for which the GC had long been renowned. The evening rush began when the second Brackley train departed at 4.55 and ended nearly two hours later when the 6.43 all stations to Gerrards Cross was given the right-away. In between there were 13 departures, with no fewer than six trains leaving at approximately 4min intervals between 5.16 and 5.30. This 14-minute burst of activity was the station's busiest spell of the whole day.

Trains on both routes were normally made up to five coaches, though regularly strengthened at peak times. The vehicles were without exception bogie coaches, thus giving a much smoother ride than the six wheelers encountered so often on other parts of the GC at that time. In addition the compartments were roomy, comfortably upholstered and electrically lit. Most of the stock had been built in late GCR days and was to remain on these services until well into the LNER period, although shortly after Grouping a set of high-roofed non-corridor Gresley coaches was noted in use on the High Wycombe service, probably on trial. In 1930 some Gresley articulated twin sets were supplied, and from about 1935 there was talk of wholesale replacement when a start was made in transferring some of the GC bogie sets to Manchester to take the place of scrapped six-wheelers, but this scheme does not seem to have been fully implemented in the years up to the war. With the continuing use of Robinson locomotives, the services thus retained their GC character to a considerable degree.

Apart from some coaches based at Aylesbury, all the suburban stock was centred on Marylebone, where extensive cleaning and washing facilities were housed in a large shed. This was situated on the up side of the line at no great distance from the platform ends, and this proximity was of considerable help in the manoeuvring of stock. All

carriage-washing was originally done by hand; a proposal for an automatic carriage-washing plant was discussed about 1929, but it is not clear whether such an apparatus was installed. During the 1930s about 15 sets of stock were needed to operate the full range of services, with a substantial pool of spare vehicles in reserve for busy times.

Life in the suburban links at Neasden Loco offered considerable variety, with the regular drivers having full road knowledge of both the GW and Metropolitan lines and also working the Brackley jobs. In 1934 one of the Brackley turns was able to claim the distinction of being the longest diagram worked by an LNER suburban tank engine, the overall distance totalling 259 miles when light engine trips were included. Another very long diagram, 257 miles altogether, took in separate workings to Sudbury, Princes Risborough, High Wycombe, and twice to Chesham, the engine being at work from 5.40am until twenty to midnight. Such intensive working could only be achieved by providing coaling facilities at Marylebone in order to cut out the otherwise necessary visits to Neasden shed, and for this purpose a rather rickety wooden stage was positioned in the approaches to the terminus on the up side. After some years of service this was replaced in 1937 by a small mechanical coaling device located on the opposite side of the line.

A very large number of crews was needed to operate the suburban services, and this meant that many drivers finished their time on this work, either remaining on it out of choice as some did, or else unable to advance because of the very limited number of places in the main line links. Thus a good many Neasden men became particularly associated with the suburban trains over long years of working them; they included Percy Hands, Sam Arrand, 'Razor' Smith, Bill Collins, Ted Harrison, the brothers Pat and Tim Sheehan, 'Snowy' Norris, George Collins, and Drivers Hart, Stevens, Pratt and Eastaff.

Aylesbury Loco, playing a small but important role in the suburban services, had the distinction of being Neasden's only sub-shed. Standing adjacent to the station, the small building was shared with the GWR and housed three LNER engines. Two of these were 'A5s' for use on the shed's turns to Marylebone, with five sets of men being involved. In 1925 the engines were booked to come off the shed at 6.45 and 7.15am for their first trip to Marylebone, after which they remained in traffic all day; they were mostly confined to Metropolitan line trains, but worked an odd trip on the GW Joint Line. On both diagrams relief crews took over at Aylesbury station.

The third Aylesbury engine was used on the motor train service to Quainton Road and Verney Junction, doing about half a dozen trips in the course of a rather leisurely diagram lasting about 13 hours. This service had an interesting early history, being worked in GCR days by a steam railcar; referred to in official GC publications as 'Steam Rail Motor Coaches', these vehicles had at one time been popular with the company, and there were at least two at work in the Neasden district. However they fell out of favour soon after World War 1, probably because of insufficient power, and were withdrawn from service. In their stead, push-and-pull units were introduced, and the coach bodies of the withdrawn railcars were converted for use as driving trailers on the new units, which went into service both on the Verney Junction train and at Woodford. The engines used on these push-and-pull sets were ex-MSJ&A 2-4-0 tanks, transferred south because the increasing weight of the Manchester suburban trains was getting too much for them. Of Sacre origin, these machines were very much at the veteran stage by this time, and although surviving into LNER ownership they did not last long enough to be renumbered. The last to go was No 450B, withdrawn at the close of 1924; shortly before its withdrawal it was sent to Stratford Works to have its push-and-pull gear transferred to its successor on the Verney Junction train. This engine, ex-GE Class F7 2-4-2T No 8307, arrived in the Neasden district in December 1924 and must almost certainly claim the honour of being the first 'foreigner' to be stationed in that part of the GC. It evidently gave satisfaction in its new role, and worked regularly on the Verney Junction service until the latter was withdrawn in July 1936. It did not entirely monopolise the train however, having several different partners over the years. Ex-GN railcar No 2, seen at Neasden and believed in use on the Verney Junction service in 1925, was probably the most unusual. Rather less out of the ordinary, though not particularly common at the southern end of the GC, was a Class F1 tank transferred from Manchester; this was No 5575, which had a stay of four months after arriving in September 1927. In January 1929 No 5594 of the same class took over and had a much longer spell, having outlasted the Verney Junction service by the time it departed in 1937. Yet another 'F1', No 5727, came south in 1933 and also lasted until 1937.

The push-and-pull diagram began at 6.40am with a trip to Quainton Road and back, then came a working to High Wycombe via the Little Kimble-Princes Risborough line; after this there were trips to Verney Junction until the day ended at 7.50pm. Two sets of men were employed.

A fairly busy service was operated on the GW&GC Joint Aylesbury-Princes Risborough line, but worked entirely by the GWR apart from the solitary morning trip by the Verney Junction motor train. When the latter was withdrawn it is believed that the push-and-pull set was used more extensively on the Princes Risborough line, as the motor-fitted Class F7 engine was still operating from Aylesbury when the war began.

Aylesbury drivers who worked on the Marylebone services before 1939 include Bob Parrott, Harry Buckingham, Bob Smith, Jack Pedley, Harry Bloxham and Fred Woodcock. The motor train was the preserve of Sam James, Joe Sales and Joe Burgess, although on Saturday evenings it was taken over by a Neasden crew to be worked empty to the parent shed for washing-out and other attention. This explains why the engine was to be seen at Neasden Loco on Sundays, as a number of photographs testify. In order to give the 'A5s' the regular weekly service at Neasden, they were sent to Aylesbury in rotation.

In November 1937 the absorption of the Metropolitan Railway into the London Passenger Transport Board took effect, with the LNER taking control over the former Metropolitan steam services north of Rickmansworth. The Metropolitan men were not displaced however, remaining in their own links and even continuing to wear their own distinctive uniform; they were proud of their origins and liked to refer to themselves as 'Met men'. In 1939 there was a passenger link of about 18 turns as well as a goods link. The main changes occurred in the locomotive field, with the transfer of the handsome Metropolitan engines to the GC shed, and subsequent closure and demolition of the Met shed a short distance away on the up side of the main line. The Class H 4-4-4 tanks continued to be used on passenger work, running light the whole distance to Rickmansworth and back to start and finish work, and it was not until after the outbreak of war that they were replaced by the 'A5s'. To work the Chesham branch however, 'C14s' Nos 6125/6/7 arrived at Neasden in January 1938, coming south for the first time since the departure of No 6125 13 years before. However they did not stay very long and were replaced by Class N5 0-6-2 tanks, which were a rather more familiar type because of the shunting work they did at Neasden and Marylebone.

Metropolitan men involved in the 1937 transfer included Drivers East, Harris, Goodman, King, Saggers, Hyde, Bishop, Kenningdale, Francis and Rowley.

A number of minor accidents occurred on the Marylebone suburban services between the wars, but none were of a really serious nature. There were several rear-end collisions, and in a few of these one of the contributory causes was the colour-light signalling that had been introduced by A. F. Bound in late GCR days. Special rules governed the observance of these signals, and under a regulation known as 'stop and proceed' it was permissible to pass them at danger after a wait of one minute; not entirely surprisingly, this led to occasional collisions. One of the more serious happened at Canfield Place in the late evening of Sunday 31 August 1924 when the 11.52pm suburban train from Wembley Hill to Marylebone headed by 'A5' No 451 struck the rear of 'B7' No 458, standing light at a signal, and catapulted it into the back of another train waiting immediately ahead; Driver Eastaff, in charge of No 451, had passed a signal in the approved manner, but had failed to proceed with sufficient caution subsequently. A considerable amount of damage to the locomotives and coaches was caused, but there were no injuries.

A somewhat similar occurrence took place at Kilburn on 2 April 1934 when 'A5' No 5156, running light into Marylebone to commence work, struck the rear of a special from Nottingham waiting at signals. The rear coach was badly damaged, but fortunately it was unoccupied and the guard had had time to jump clear as he saw the approaching bunker of No 5156. The only injuries were to the driver of the 'A5', Walter Stevens, who was in hospital for a month afterwards; the accident was caused by his failure to observe the signals properly. There was an element of providence in this mishap, for the damaged coach had contained a number of passengers who only a few moments before the impact had decided to go forward through the corridor to save walking-time at Marylebone; they happened to be a party of religious revivalists on their way to a rally at the Albert Hall (the day was Easter Monday), and on discovering their remarkably lucky escape they knelt down on the spot and gave thanks to the Almighty!

Apart from the suicides which occasionally take place on all railways, fatalities of any kind were almost unknown. A very rare and somewhat strange case occurred on 31 October 1923, when a late-evening train from Aylesbury arrived in Marylebone with a dead body hanging out of one of the windows; the head was badly battered, and it transpired that the individual concerned, a newspaper employee on his way to work, had been leaning too far out of the window and his head had struck a bridge abutment.

A well-known Neasden driver, Ted Harrison, lost his life on 6 August 1936 when he fell from the footplate of his engine at Sudbury Hill while working the 6.58pm Marylebone-Ruislip train.

An examination of the suburban timetables current at July 1939 shows that the GW Joint Line service had continued to expand. The number of Monday-to-Friday departures from Marylebone for this route had risen from 31 to 45, while the Aylesbury service had remained the same. There was a similar increase in up trains and in the Saturday service. The continuing growth of this traffic was due to building development in the districts served; the population of High Wycombe, given as 22,000 in the mid-1920s, had risen to over 30,000 by the end of the next decade. However the absence of locomotive stabling facilities at the down end of the route, such as existed at Aylesbury, was an operating handicap and resulted in much light engine running between Neasden and High Wycombe. Stock of certain late-evening trains was stored overnight in a siding, but space appears to have been limited. In the mornings two light engines left Neasden and proceeded to High Wycombe for the 6.55 and 7.30am trains to Marylebone. By contrast with the exiguous facilities at High Wycombe, even Rickmansworth was comparatively well equipped. Here a small coal stage and inspection pit was provided for the engines waiting to take over northbound trains relinquished by the electrics, or returning with trains from the country; these facilities obviated a large number of otherwise inevitable light engine trips to Neasen Loco, although as indicated a certain amount of light running was unavoidable at the beginning and end of the day.

By September 1939 the 'A5' engines had run up a total of 28 years' continuous service on the Marylebone suburban trains, and still had a long way to go. Their prowess had also been made known in other parts, particularly on the GN Section after certain members of the class had worked for a time at Kings Cross and in the West Riding. Apart from the short-lived employment of Class N7 engines described earlier, and occasional assistance from the 'Crabs' at busy times, they had no rivals. In the spring of 1938 an unidentified Class N2 engine was observed shunting the Metropolitan coal sidings at Stanmore, but in all probability this engine would have been on temporary loan to Neasden as at this time the former Metropolitan engines were being overhauled at Stratford Works. The 'A5s' are thus one of the very few Gorton-designed passenger types which in the years between the wars remained on the work for which they had been originally built.

55

In between turns. 'A5' No 447 stands on Neasden shed not long after Grouping. In the background are the GC wagon repair shops, largely destroyed by a flying bomb during World War 2. *Authors' Collection*

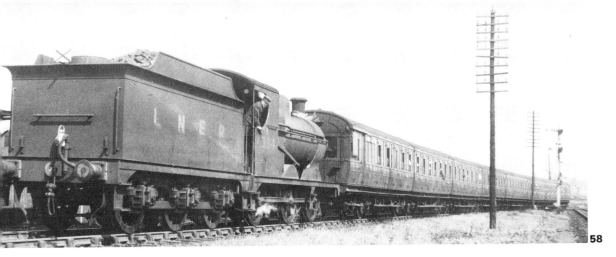

58

56
'J62' No 5886 at Staveley Loco in prewar days. Sister engine No 885 was at Neasden for a time in connection with the Exhibition. *G. Coltas*

57
Wembley Stadium station on 4 July 1928. 'A5' No 452C is about to depart for Marylebone, carrying the distinctive 'Wembley Loop' identification board in the form of a St Andrew's Cross. The array of vintage advertisements on the hoarding contrasts with the ornate style of architecture, the latter of course associated with the British Empire Exhibition of a few years before. *H. C. Casserley*

58
A postwar view of the Wembley Loop with 'J11' No 4394 coming off the main line with a trainload of football fans, possibly for the 1949 Cup Final. The Wembley Loop identification board is again visible, and the all-Gresley stock will be noted. *C. R. L. Coles*

59
Chesham on 8 April 1933, with 'A5' No 5449 preparing to leave with a Marylebone train. One of the Robinson anti-collision fenders may be seen on the coach next to the engine. *W. Potter*

59

60
'F1' No 5594 shows the characteristic lines of a small GCR suburban tank engine during its Sunday call at Neasden Loco. *Courtesy GCRS*

61
With an 'F1' at the head, the Aylesbury motor train was a highly typical GC ensemble, and one that would have been instantly familiar to visitors from the Manchester end of the system. No 5594 departs from Aylesbury in 1929. *G. Coltas*

62
No 5594 arrives at Quainton Road with the 3.30pm Verney Junction-Aylesbury train on 6 May 1935. *W. Potter*

63
'Push-and-pull'. 'F7' No 8307 is sandwiched between coaches during a call at Princes Risborough, with the distinctive GCR 12-wheeler nearest the camera. *G. Coltas*

64
No 107 of Metropolitan Class H is seen on the Metropolitan
shed at Neasden about 1930. The Metropolitan power
station is visible in the background. *G. Coltas*

65
A year after Grouping, but little has changed in this
photograph of No 450B at Aylesbury, actually taken on
19 January 1924. Within a short time these engines had
disappeared for good. *W. Potter*

66

66
Bunker-first working was an integral part of life in the
suburban link. 'A5' No 5046 near Ruislip and Ickenham with
a train for Marylebone in the 1930s. *Real Photographs*

67
No 5006, one of the last batch of 'A5s', accelerates out of
Marylebone in the 1920s. The coal stage used by suburban
engines can be seen at left. *Real Photographs*

67

6

68
Northwood on a Bank Holiday weekend in the 1930s. 'L1' No 5340 is at work on an empty stock train. *B. K. Cooper*

69
The 'C14s' reappeared on the Marylebone suburban scene after an absence of many years. No 6125 was photographed at Ipswich on 24 August 1938.
R. W. Todd courtesy Gresley Society

70
Another Manchester exile was 'F1' No 5727, seen here on Neasden Loco in the mid-1930s. *Authors' Collection*

71
'L1' No 5342 is at Rickmansworth on goods work, this being the usual role of the class. A picture taken in the late 1930s. *B. K. Cooper*

7

72
'A5' No 448 prepares to leave Ruislip and Ickenham with a
Marylebone train in 1924.
F. R. Hebron/Rail Archive Stephenson

73
'A5' No 5449 takes water at Ruislip troughs while working
the 5.5pm Marylebone-Brackley train in 1935; this was one
of the longest diagrams worked by suburban engines
anywhere in Britain.
F. R. Hebron/Rail Archive Stephenson

'A5' No 5158 passes Northolt Park on a Marylebone-High
Wycombe train, 1938. *C. R. L. Coles*

An unidentified Metropolitan Class H engine on a down train
at Aylesbury in the 1930s. Aylesbury loco shed may be seen
in the right background. *Authors' Collection*

76
Metropolitan in the country. Class H No 107 at Verney
Junction in 1935. *Photomatic*

77
Class H No 108 is uncoupling from an up train at
Rickmansworth for the electric to take over.
Real Photographs

77

Part Three: Animal and Mineral
9 Woodhead Coal Traffic

Recently closed at the time of writing, the Woodhead route in its heyday could undoubtedly claim to be the most important artery on the whole Great Central system, with a line-occupation as dense as any in the country except for the very congested routes in the vicinity of London. Incorporating some of the most severe gradients encountered on British main lines, it took its name from what was throughout LNER days the fourth longest tunnel in the country, and from a staff point of view probably the most unpleasant to pass through. It was a line of contrasts. Reaching an altitude of 1,000ft at Dunford Bridge, the line here was set amid surroundings which have been most aptly described by George Dow — 'bleak and desolate beyond words in winter'. Yet it offered some of the most attractive scenery to be found in the north of England, particularly on the western side, although as earlier chapters have made clear, it was liable at any time of the winter to be affected by the most severe weather conditions.

Geographically speaking, it linked Lancashire and Yorkshire, wandering somewhat vaguely along the border of Cheshire and Derbyshire in the region between Woodhead and Guide Bridge — the location of Woodhead, sometimes erroneously described as Yorkshire or even Lancashire, was actually Cheshire under the county boundaries in existence during LNER days, although a more untypical part of that county would be difficult to imagine. The interest of this western side of the hill was enhanced by two other prominent engineering features, the viaducts at Dinting Vale and Broadbottom, which were among the most impressive structures on the system. Rising to a height of 120ft, they remain spectacular monuments to the early days of railway enterprise, and are prominent local landmarks. Their correct names are Dinting Vale viaduct and Besthill viaduct, but these original titles are seldom used and they have been known to generations of local residents as 'Dinting Arches' and 'Broadbottom Arches'. These names are of historical interest inasmuch as they hint at the curved shape of the original wooden members, the later structures not being arches in the correct sense of the word.

Extended by various stages during the early 1840s, the Woodhead route proper may be said to have come into existence with the completion of the first bore of Woodhead tunnel in 1845, this historic event being marked by an appropriate ceremony. From a traffic point of view the early history of the line is obscure, but it is clear that it soon became a trunk route for the conveyance of coal westwards across the Pennines. During the 19th century the mines in the Barnsley area, many directly accessible from what was then the MS&L system, were at their peak of production, and fortunes were being made from the buying and selling of coal. The bulk of this went to Lancashire, where the cotton trade was then one of the wonders of the industrial world, and further demand came from the ports of Merseyside and the development of a heavy engineering industry in Manchester. All this created an ever-increasing traffic in coal along the Woodhead line, and the completion of a second bore alongside the original in 1852 was doubtless a much-needed improvement.

The continuing growth of traffic after this date called for further increase in capacity, of which the most valuable would have been complete quadrupling of the track throughout; alas this was ruled out for reasons of expense, and instead the company contented itself with installing loop accommodation in successive stages. Increases in traffic quickly swallowed up the effect of each improvement, and when at the end of the century the declining output of some of the older Barnsley pits seemed likely to exert an adverse influence, the sinking of new and very much larger mines further east and in Nottinghamshire ensured that business would continue to boom. By this time the Woodhead coal traffic had become a major problem for the Great Central, as the company had by then become, and there was obviously no easy solution. The only real advance during the next few years was a degree of speeding-up as a result of the running of longer trains, this deriving from the introduction of eight-coupled mineral engines under the designer J. G. Robinson. Coming as late as 1902, this development seems in retrospect a little overdue; prior to this date it was presumably necessary to make use of an assistant engine to work the 60-wagon trains known as 'double-loads', if such were ever worked at all, and it is possible that the lack of a suitable type of engine before the turn of the century may have been one of the reasons why Robinson's predecessor, the influential Harry Pollitt, lost favour with the management. From 1902 onward the 'double-load' became the more usual Woodhead coal train, and this was the form which was to remain so familiar during LNER days.

The problems which afflicted the coal traffic were however rather too deep-seated for the use of more powerful engines to be anything more than a drop in the bucket. The chief difficulties arose from the conjunction of severe gradients and absence of sufficient mileage of quadruple track to keep the mineral trains completely clear of the faster services. Woodhead Tunnel itself was the most serious bottleneck, with only a single road in each direction for a distance of three miles; invariably there was a queue of trains waiting to pass through, and at both ends extra roads had to be installed to provide standage room for trains held up, sometimes for days, in order to keep the line clear for more important traffic. A further huge problem was the sorting of wagons; a vast conglomeration of privately-owned vehicles was perpetually en route for a wide spread of destinations west of Woodhead, and in the reverse direction all these had to be sorted and returned to the colliery from which they originated. Marshalling of both loaded and empty wagons was thus a literally never-ending process, with thousands of man and engine-hours consumed weekly in this task alone.

An important step was taken in 1907 with the opening of the new and ultra-modern marshalling yard at Wath. More properly termed a concentration yard, this installation was one of the country's showpieces at the time of its opening, greatly speeding-up the formation of trains and simplifying the working of trips to and from the collieries. Unfortunately however the much accelerated sorting rate at Wath could not make its full contribution without a similar installation west of the Pennines, since each train required further marshalling before reaching its destination; hence the more rapid sorting in Yorkshire simply led to a greater build-up of waiting traffic. The facilities for marshalling which existed on the western side were centred at Godley and Guide Bridge, and despite the most intensive round-the-clock working neither place was really adequately equipped to deal with such a dense traffic. Thus it became usual to find every single loop between Guide Bridge and Woodhead, if not indeed beyond, occupied by a coal train waiting to leapfrog its way for a short distance along the main line. So severe were the delays that at weekends the trains were often left standing in the loops with brakes pinned down, the engines being released and sent light to Gorton; this was apt to cause other problems, for wagons left on the more isolated stretch east of Hadfield were frequently a prey to pilferers. The congestion reached particularly serious proportions in the boom years immediately following World War 1, when it became common for drivers to spend an entire shift without moving, being eventually relieved by men sent out to the spot. The only cure for such problems, as the GCR well knew, was the provision of a modern marshalling yard west of Woodhead, but alas this was not to be forthcoming until 1935, when Mottram Yard was eventually opened.

Up to this date therefore, the Woodhead coal traffic was bedevilled by virtually every operating problem which a railway service could possibly suffer from, and as though this were not enough, the most serious dislocation could be caused at any time by the state of the weather. In the days before smoke control legislation the Manchester area was subject to industrial fogs dense enough to bring traffic to a complete standstill, and which could sometimes last for days. Between November and April the icy grip of winter would often be felt on the more elevated stretch of line between Barnsley Junction and Hadfield, freezing points and signals, often reducing visibility to a few yards, and in really severe weather blocking the line altogether; in such conditions enginemen, guards and line staff often battled in vain to keep the coal trains moving.

The discomforts which winter caused the staff can probably be better visualised by those familiar with the district. Study of newspapers and conversation with retired railwaymen from the area reveal the fact that prewar winters were somewhat more severe than seems to have been the case in more recent times, and the hardships of working at such extremely exposed locations as the yard at Dunford Bridge may not be readily realised. In severe weather the Dunford staff had to work for hours on end in sub-zero temperatures, with visibility often restricted by blizzards, and the ever-present danger created by treacherous conditions underfoot, while an additional burden of work had to be coped with in the fight to keep points and pointwork from freezing. Their only respite was the opportunity to escape into one of the not very warm cabins during a lull in traffic. For footplatemen and guards the only escape was in the gradual downhill progress towards warmer regions, the difference in temperature between Dunford and Dinting being at times amazing; probably it was the guards who suffered the most, for whereas the engine crews at least had the heat of the firebox, the former could only huddle round the tiny 'Gorton Stove', stuffing newspapers in the doors to block the icy draughts; their discomforts were further increased by the frequent need to leave their vans in order to attend to wagon brakes, or to make various signals.

Personal risk, never entirely absent from any form of railway work, was particularly evident in much of the work associated with the Woodhead traffic, whatever the time of year. For yard staff a false step could have tragic consequences, and the difficulty of hearing approaching trains during spells of windy weather demanded exceptional caution. For enginemen and guards the most serious danger was that of trains getting out of control on the gradients, the two main causes of this being a failure of the engine brakes or breakage of wagon couplings leading to what was sometimes called a 'run-back'. The only safeguard against such happenings was the exercise of both skill and vigilance at both ends of the train. The danger of a complete train running away was guarded against as far as possible by the practice of pinning down a certain number of wagon brakes at the top of the western descent; guards also put on their own brakes as firmly as possible, but of course the pull of 60 loaded coal wagons would considerably exceed even this combination of brake-power if the engine brakes were out of the reckoning. From the 1920s onwards some of the eight-wheel brake-vans of Great Northern origin were used on the Woodhead trains, but as their total weight was only 20 tons they were not really a great advance on the GC six-wheel type. On the western descent from Woodhead therefore, the coal trains were notable for their extremely low speed; Mr S. C. Townroe has recorded how, when he was on the footplate of the Class O4 engine waiting with a loaded train, he was severely rebuked by the driver for opening the regulator as the signal was pulled off, being sharply informed that the weight of the train would be quite sufficient to push them forward on the downgrade.

As an ultimate safeguard, the loop adjacent to Valehouse box led to a sand-drag which ended close to the next box at Hadfied East. During MSL days there are believed to have been quite a number of runaways, and one is also known to have occurred about 1912 which resulted in derailment of a train and damage to the engine at Hadfield East. However such happenings seem to have grown less and less frequent as time went on, probably as a result of operating experience and improvements in equipment, and during LNER days they appear to have been very rare. The vigilance of staff would probably have been increased following the accident which took place at Sprotborough in the spring of 1924, when the rear portion of a goods train broke away on a rising gradient and ran back to collide with a following train; the guard had failed to keep a look-out, and the result of his negligence was that he and two others riding in the van were killed, a fourth man being severely injured. Such a salutary lesson would not have been lost on the Woodhead guards.

Many stories have been told of the dangers of suffocating when making the passage of Woodhead Tunnel. The experience of slogging through three miles of single-bore tunnel on a heavily-loaded mineral engine is not likely to have been a pleasant one, but in all probability the stories of crews collapsing on the footplate have little foundation in fact, although it should be remembered that at about the time of World War 1 the ventilation had been improved by the addition of several new shafts, and prior to this the conditions may well have been bad enough to cause considerable suffering to men affected by the bronchial ailments which still remain all too common in the north-west. The most serious danger inside the tunnels, by far, was to lengthmen and other line staff, and there were a number of cases of men being run down; one of the chief difficulties in such cases of course was the crew's complete lack of vision — a factor which could produce other curious aberrations, such as the occasion during World War 2 when the driver of a passenger train mistook his direction and propelled the train backwards out of the tunnel.

Apart from the death, injury and discomfort which it caused to staff, the tunnel also cost the company thousands of pounds in maintenance. The two bores had been driven in such a way that the summit of the climb was close to the eastern exit, and this meant that the up tunnel recieved a continual pounding day and night as engines struggled over the top. The blast dislodged mortar and loosened stonework, and although repair work was frequently carried out the damage soon recurred. This problem became progressively more acute during LNER days, with the up tunnel sometimes being completely closed on Sundays to enable the necessary work to be carried out; in spite of all efforts the fabric of the tunnel continued to deteriorate, and it was this which eventually led, in postwar years, to the decision to abandon the original bores in favour of a new tunnel.

Against this catalogue of difficulties there was not a great deal to set on the credit side. One small improvement was in the wagon position. In pre-Grouping days the up yard at Dunford was largely devoted to the task of sorting private owners' empties brought up 'rough' from Lancashire, and this totally unproductive activity had long been recognised as a complete drain on time and resources, adding enormously to the cost of the operations. Unfortunately it was a situation which the company was powerless to remedy, but it so happened that during the 1920s the fortunes of the coal companies declined somewhat, which resulted in a number of mergers and amalgamations, while in some cases pooling arrangements were entered into; all this was of help in cutting down the amount of marshalling of empties and was thus welcomed by the LNER, although of course there is no doubt that they would have liked to go much further and scrap the system altogether in favour of a comprehensive pooling scheme. Had such a plan been put into effect it would have done away with unproductive marshalling and probably had some effect in improving standards of maintenance of the wagons, which were often kept in traffic in a serious state of disrepair because of the owners' neglect; it was not unknown for private-owner wagons to collapse completely during marshalling. From the observer's point of view the effect of the amalgamations was to reduce the very wide variety of differently-painted wagons which made the coal trains of that era such an attractive sight; only the names of the bigger or more prosperous concerns continued to apear, these including Elsecar, Monckton, Wath Main, Denaby, Maltby, Rother Vale, Sheepbridge, Bolsover and Newstead, to mention only a few. In addition to these, which were coal-producing firms there were a number of prominent coal distributors owning their own wagons, such as Stephenson Clarke, E. & F. Beattie, and Settle Speakman.

The only development which could be described as a real improvement to the Woodhead coal traffic in these years was the opening of the marshalling yard at Mottram in 1935. It would require a separate chapter to deal adequately with this subject, and it must suffice here to say that it was capable of carrying out all the marshalling which had previously been done at Godley and Guide Bridge, and in far less time, thus amply fulfilling its primary function; congestion in the Woodhead loops was greatly reduced and the trains were kept moving, although by this time, alas, the traffic was falling off to some extent and the yard often worked below its full capacity.

The story of what happened to so much of the coal industry between the wars will be well-known to most readers, and only the barest detail can be given here. The depressed state of trade, the technological changes which were beginning to make heavy industry less dependent on the traditional coal-fired furnace, the more economical use of coal in both home and factory, perhaps also the psychological effect of the many coal strikes following World War 1 — all these things were cutting down the consumption of coal at a gradually increasing rate, and by 1935 the process was already well advanced. It was not until the stimulus of the war effort began to be felt that Mottram Yard was able to prove its real worth.

So far as locomotive developments are concerned there was not a great deal of change in the period under review. The traffic was dominated by what was surely J. G. Robinson's best design — the Class 8K 2-8-0. Introduced in 1911 as a development of the original '8A' 0-8-0, the

'Tinies' as they came to be known quickly came to prominence on all the GC mineral services, and their position was to remain pretty well unchallenged until after World War 2. To some extent this dominance was a the result of the LNER's decision to purchase a large number of Government-owned examples shortly after Grouping; these had originally been built for war service, and their addition to LNER stock brought the total of the class, now known as 'O4', up to more than 400. Large allocations of these engines were maintained at Gorton and Mexborough, the two sheds most directly involved with the Woodhead traffic, which totalled about 120 of the type altogether. 'O4s' from a wide variety of other sheds were also to be regularly seen on coal trains over Woodhead, these including Doncaster, Sheffield, Frodingham, Immingham, Staveley, Annesley and Colwick. The 'O4s' were supported by their older cousins the 0-8-0s, although by the beginning of the LNER period the latter had been transferred away from the most important 'coal' sheds and were mainly concentrated at Barnsley and Langwith, with a few at Doncaster and Frodingham; despite the fact that one or two of the class were condemned as early as 1934 they continued to play a modest part in the Woodhead coal service. All 'double-loads' were invariably handled by eight-coupled types, and apart from a very occasional appearance of an NER engine the two native designs monopolised the service.

For the lighter trains, the 'single-loads' as they were called, 0-6-0 engines were sometimes used, and without any doubt the most popular were the 'Pom-poms' — officially Class J11 in the LNER list but much better known by their unusual nickname because they had first come into service at the time when the pom-pom gun was used by the Boers during the South African War. Age seemed to make no difference to the capacity of these versatile machines, which were capable of tackling every kind of assignment apart from the heaviest mineral and passenger trains. Their use on the shorter coal trains carried the advantage that they could be diagrammed for almost any kind of job on the return trip, though they were in fact capable of taking quite substantial trains of empties when necessary; a photo taken at Valehouse in 1939 shows No 5302, of Heaton Mersey shed, working an exceptionally lengthy string of empties.

An 0-6-0 type which became progressively more popular as time went by was the LNER-designed 'J39', which proved itself the equal of the 'Pom-pom' and came to enjoy much the same esteem among the crews. At first, appearances of this type were rare because only a small number were allocated to sheds involved in the coal service, but as time went on they came to take an increasing share of the traffic.

East of Dunford the presence of banking engines added to the locomotive variety, as at busy times almost any type would be turned out for this duty. As a rule the double-loads were banked by 'O4s', but single-loads would bring 'Pom-poms', 'J39s', or whatever kind of engine Mexborough happened to have handy. A type which did an increasing amount of this kind of work during the 1930s was the Class L1 'Crab'; these engines

had proved a failure on main-line work because of a tendency to skid when braking, and between Grouping and the war they were tried in various experimental roles. Their biggest success, undoubtedly, was banking coal trains from Wath up to Dunford; no fewer than seven of the class were sent to Mexborough early in 1929 especially for this purpose, and others followed in 1933. Being large and powerful machines they were very suitable as bankers, and the extra protection afforded by their cabs made them popular with the Mexborough men. Trains coming from the Mansfield and Worksop areas were sometimes banked by former LDECR tank engines, although here again there was considerable variety to be observed.

The coal was destined for the furnaces of a huge variety of mills and factories, stretching from the Glossop area through to Liverpool and the Wirral. The first wagons to reach their destination, in point of distance, were those bound for Padfield Mills, these premises being accessible from a spur which left the down line a short distance below Hadfield East signalbox. However, like other mills in the Glossop area, the ones at Padfield fell on hard times with the decline of the cotton trade from the early 1920s; this was particularly true of the Waterside Branch, just beyond Dinting Arches, for whereas at one period this had served as many as six different mills in Hadfield and Tintwistle, its traffic gradually shrank to a trickle.

The first major calling-point was Godley, where trains bound for Stockport and the CLC system were remarshalled as necessary; these included trains for Liverpool, the cargo either to be used as ships' bunkers or to go for export. Trains bound for the Manchester area were broken up at Guide Bridge, except for those rather rare specimens which were able to continue through to their destination as block loads. The huge volume of marshalling at Guide Bridge involved round-the-clock working for several pilot engines as the mineral trains were split up and combined with other traffic, then taken away in trip workings to various points. All this of course disappeared with the opening of Mottram Yard in 1935.

A good proportion of the coal was supplied to merchants for domestic use or delivery to factories not directly linked with the railway. In the goods yard of most stations the office of the local coal merchant was usually to be found, and he normally leased a siding or else a part of the 'coal drops' if the station was equipped with such. At more important stations several merchants would have a share in the traffic, and during the day the yard would be a hive of continual activity as lorries and horse-drawn drays came and went, taking loads of coal either to local factories and other premises, or else piled high with the well-known hundredweight bags for domestic delivery. The coal merchants were a variegated group of entrepreneurs, some operating on a small scale with a single owner-driven vehicle, others employing gangs of men in the coal sidings and having a virtual monopoly of coal deliveries over a wide area. These more prosperous operators often acted as agents for particular colliery companies. Local Co-operative Societies were very active in the business of domestic supply, and many householders in the Manchester area had their coal delivered by the 'Co-op'. At the upper end of the scale were undertakings such as that of E. & F. Beattie, whose yard on the down side of the main line opposite Ardwick station, known as the 'Kobo Sidings', consisted of no fewer than four roads and at busy times provided plenty of work for a pilot engine; the sidings were unusual in being situated well below the level of the main line, the access road descending a steep ramp at the Manchester end.

Plans for electrification of the Woodhead line were discussed as early as 1926, although little is known of them beyond the fact that certain tests were carried out in June and July 1927 to gain information as to the traction requirements. Of relevance to the present chapter is the test conducted on Friday 8 July, when 'O5' No 5414 worked a 473-ton train of coal empties from Dewsnap Yard to Dunford Bridge. After a signal stop at Hyde Junction, where the up loop from Dewsnap joins the main line, the train reached Crowden in just over an hour, which by the standards of those days was rather good going. After a halt here the train was held, somewhat more typically, by adverse signals in two separate places at Woodhead before finally getting into the tunnel; it negotiated this in just over eight minutes — apparently without slipping, which suggests an experienced hand at the regulator. It is no doubt significant that for this test the large-boilered Class O5 2-8-0 was preferred to the much more common 'O4'. Following the trials the electrification project seems to have fallen into abeyance, probably because the LNER were not prepared to part with the money, but during the thirties the scheme was resurrected, and a large Government loan voted late in 1935 ensured that it would go ahead. Work is believed to have been started in 1938, but was then suspended on the outbreak of war. By this time a number of stanchions had been erected on the section between Woodhead and Hadfield, painted in bright red lead, and after fears had been voiced that these would aid navigation of enemy aircraft a gang of men was hurriedly put to work to paint them black. In view of statements to the effect that the electrification was planned in conjunction with the driving of the new tunnel, it should perhaps be pointed out that under the original scheme the wires were to be carried through the existing single bores, the decision to construct a new tunnel being a much later development.

Had it been possible to complete the electrification before the war, it is likely that the greatly increased speed and efficiency of working would have helped the LNER to stave off the effects of growing competition from the road hauliers, which by 1939 was beginning to make itself felt in the realm of coal haulage. But as in so many other respects, the company was out of luck, and when eventually the work of electrification was resumed under British Railways auspices, the potential threat from road competition was much greater than it had been in the 1930s.

78
'Hitting the Hole'. A rare view of the down end of Woodhead tunnels taken from the footplate of 'J11' No 5986 on 24 July 1931 by Immingham fireman Bill Botham; he was returning home from his first-ever lodging turn in Manchester. *W. Botham*

85

79
Climbing to Woodhead. The fireman can be seen in action as an immaculate 'O4' No 6613 approaches Torside on up coal empties in the late 1930s. Rhodeswood Reservoir forms the background. *R. E. Grundy/Author's Collection*

80
'O4' No 6559 is at Dunford with a typical Woodhead mineral train bound for Lancashire. *R. E. Grundy/Authors' Collection*

81
On the last lap of the climb. 'O4' No 6190 struggles away
from Dunford towards the tunnel with a train of Stephenson
Clarke wagons, at some date in the 1930s.
R. E. Grundy/Authors' Collection

82
A well-earned rest. 'O4' No 6186 takes water in the down
sidings at Dunford; a 1930s view.
R. E. Grundy/Authors' Collection

82

83

'Single-load'. 'J11' No 5255 is seen in the vicinity of Hazlehead Bridge as it climbs towards Woodhead in the late 1920s. The presence of Hickleton and Wath Main wagons indicates a train from Yorkshire.
R. E. Grundy/Authors' Collection

84

'J11' No 5255 again on 1 June 1939. It has exchanged its Robinson chimney for the LNER type, and is seen shunting at Godley. *A. Appleton*

85
The murk and smoke of Woodhead tunnel are well conveyed in this picture, taken below the overbridge at Dunford, as an unidentified 'J39' heads east with a mixed goods in the 1930s. *R. E. Grundy/Authors' Collection*

86
Waiting for the road. Engines queueing up to enter the tunnel were a familiar sight at Woodhead. An unidentified 'O4' waits with steam up in the 1930s.
R. E. Grundy/Authors' Collection

87
The engine of the 1927 test. 'O5' No 5414 is seen at Retford Loco, where it was based for many years. The picture was taken in about 1931. *G. Coltas/Authors' Collection*

88
Banker. An unidentified 'O4' plods along behind a GC six-wheel brake as yet another mineral train climbs towards Woodhead. *R. E. Grundy/Authors' Collection*

89
The 'Q4s' were another class which took a good share in the Woodhead mineral workings, but were not very common as far south as Woodford, where this photograph was taken. No 5163 was a Mexborough engine in 1930, about which time it was photographed. *G. Coltas*

90
Staveley Loco had a considerable share in the Woodhead workings. Here is 'O4' No 6269 at the coaling stage about 1931. *G. Coltas*

91
The Class J11 'Pom-poms' were the best maids-of-all-work on the GC. Here is No 5287 on Retford GC Loco, in the early 1930s. Buildings on London Road may be seen in the distance, and it was in this vicinity that visiting enginemen lodged. *G. Coltas*

92
Barnsley Loco in 1938, a somewhat humble structure considering the important work that was done. It had originally been shared with the LYR, but the latter moved out after Grouping and the LNER took over the whole premises. *Ian Allan Library*

93
The work of the Class B7 'four-cylinders' is typified in this August 1945 view of an unidentified member of the class climbing above Valehouse with an up train of hoppers. The tender carries the slogan 'Vote Labour', a reminder of the general election of that year. *W. Potter*

94
Woodhead down platform in GCR days. The buildings were a superb example of vernacular architecture, echoing the rugged strength of the surrounding moorland. *Authors' Collection*

92

93

94

95
Woodhead station and village from the main Manchester-Sheffield road, in GCR days. Lying on opposite sides of the River Etherow, visible in the centre, they were in separate counties — the village in Cheshire and the station in Derbyshire. *Authors' Collection*

96
'O4' No 6184 draws into Dunford down loop with a coal train in LNER days, with the usual banker at the rear. *LPC/Rail Archive Stephenson*

10 Garratt

The belief that the Class U1 Garratt introduced in 1925 was designed specially for banking on the Worsborough incline has long been an accepted part of LNER history. This interpretation, in fact, is contradicted by a number of factors, and it is the aim of this chapter to suggest a different version of the story, and to present the history of the Garratt in a fresh perspective.

Two general considerations may be mentioned to begin with. The previous chapter has given some indication of the serious problems associated with the Woodhead coal traffic, and whilst the Worsborough bank was a considerable operating handicap it was no more of a hindrance to the smooth running of the trains than were a number of other factors, and it is most unlikely that the LNER would have gone to the trouble and expense of building a Garratt in order to achieve no greater end result than the saving of one crew at Wentworth, where the engine was based, for in normal operation it made no difference to the traffic whether the trains were banked by the Garratt or by two ordinary engines. Even the most efficient banking engine ever built would not have made any difference, and the Garratt was a long way from being in that class. Secondly, the operational use of Garratts both in Britain and elsewhere shows clearly that the type was intended as a traffic engine; if the LNER example was indeed designed as a banker then it must almost certainly have been the only one of its type that ever was; its use at Worsborough demonstrated that in a number of ways it was unsuitable as a banker.

The project which eventually crystallised as the LNER Garratt had a long history, and was bound up with various other schemes and proposals which either failed to materialise or did so only in part. To trace these it is necessary to delve into the pre-Grouping era.

The GCR designer John G. Robinson first took an active interest in the Garratt type in 1910, when he got out a scheme for a Garratt based on the Class 8A 0-8-0 design of 1902 (LNER Class Q4); this never got beyond the drawing-board stage, and almost certainly its place in the general scheme of things was taken by the well-known Class 8K 2-8-0, which appeared in the following year. This indicates that Robinson was mainly concerned with the question of building a main-line mineral engine at this time, and although little information has been traced relating to the abortive Garratt proposal there is nothing to suggest that it was ever intended as a banker.

Robinson's interest in the Garratt patent is in many ways typical of the man. The first-ever example had seen the light of day only two or three years before, in the shape of a small narrow-gauge compound Garratt built for service in Tasmania. This machine is now in the National Railway Museum at York, and as the progenitor of a famous series it enjoys a good deal more limelight nowadays than at the time of its building, its original emergence from the Beyer Peacock works having gone almost unnoticed. A second Garratt under construction about the time Robinson was considering his own variant of the type attracted much more attention than the original, receiving considerable coverage in the technical press following some assiduous promotion by the Beyer Peacock company. Ever-ready to try something new, Robinson would have taken the keenest interest in these developments.

His interest would obviously have sprung in part from the close ties between his company and Beyer Peacock's. Apart from the physical proximity described in Chapter 3, Peacock's had built a number of engines for the GCR and also supplied the company with machine tools at regular intervals; there were also personal contacts, for William Thorneley, the GCR Chief Locomotive Draughtsman and the first manager of Gorton works under Robinson, had originally come to the company from Peacock's. Probably Robinson would have had the opportunity of studying the early Garratts at first-hand, and may even have talked over his own proposal with the Peacock design staff, but the factors which caused him to abandon his scheme must remain obscure.

As is well known, the '8K' design proved an outstanding success, but this appears to have acted only as a spur towards the provision of still larger mineral engines. It has already been pointed out more than once that for the GCR the coal traffic was of the greatest importance, and of course by this time the building of Immingham had opened up still wider prospects. Robinson's aim, clearly, was to provide engines of the very maximum haulage capacity; he was presented with a challenge which he appears to have taken up with a good deal of enthusiasm.

In the event, only one of these larger locomotives was fated to see the light of day, this being the somewhat unadventurous reboilering of the '8K' which emerged in 1918 as the '8M', but the projects on the drawing-board give an insight into the way Robinson's mind was working. Two separate 2-10-2s were considered, both of which would have been a revolution in size and power had they ever materialised. Copies of the drawings can be seen in Volume III of Mr G. Dow's *Great Central*. The fact that one of these was designed by the American firm of Baldwin serves as a reminder of Robinson's interest in the transatlantic scene, and especially in locomotive power and wagon capacity. Interestingly enough a drawing of a banking engine for the Worsborough line was also got out, this being an elongated version of the 0-8-4 humping engines at work in Wath Yard; if offers an interesting comparison with the LNER Garratt.

The fact that none of these proposals for a main line mineral engine ever got beyond the drawing-board was the result of physical limitations which fall into two categories. In the first place, neither the Woodhead line nor that linking the Yorkshire coal mines with Immingham was able to take anything larger than a 2-8-0 at the time when the Baldwin scheme was looked at. And secondly there was the difficulty of firing the larger machines.

The GCR management was not to be put off by such problems, and great efforts were made to overcome them. A systematic programme of improvements was put in hand on the lines concerned, involving a whole series of major works which included the building of the Doncaster Avoiding Line, provision of a massive steel bridge across the Trent at Keadby and associated deviation railway, filling in of the arches of the Scotter Road viaduct near Frodingham, strengthening by additional piers of the Dinting and Etherow Viaducts, and provision of more efficient ventilation in the Woodhead Tunnels. Completed in the years 1915-9, these developments permitted the use of considerably heavier locomotives.

As for the firing problem, there were two ways of overcoming this. The most obvious was the adoption of mechanical stoking, and in view of Robinson's interest in American developments it is rather surprising that there is no evidence of him having considered this option. As well as reducing the exertions of the fireman, mechanical stokers made possible a greater sustained output from the locomotive, permitted the use of cheaper grades of coal, and caused less smoke. As early as September 1905, a good many years before the use of very large mineral engines was considered, the GCR staff journal carried a short article reprinted from an American magazine in which the advantages of the mechanical stoker were discussed; the following is a particularly relevant extract:

'The enormous increase in the power of locomotives means increased boiler power, and consequently a much greater width and depth of firebox. Unfortunately the increased capacity of the locomotives has not been accompanied by an increase in the capacity of the firemen. So arduous have become the duties of the fireman that the railroads have seriously considered the subject of placing two firemen on the high-powered locomotives. There is a limit to a man's physical capacity, and if attempt is made to exceed it, the result is inevitably loss of efficiency. The solution of the problem seems to be the automatic stoker.'

By 1914 mechanical stokers were well established on the other side of the Atlantic, and by the mid-1920s there were a total of 8,729 mechanically stoked locomotives in use in the USA and Canada. At this time the LNER were building Pacifics with a grate area approaching that envisaged for one of the larger mineral types, and with other companies following the trend later it is surprising that no exhaustive experiments were ever made with mechanical stokers in this country. Perhaps the later engines' more efficient use of fuel influenced the situation, which can otherwise be put down only to typical British conservatism.

The alternative method of achieving high firing rates was to convert the locomotives to a different type of fuel, and it is against this background that Robinson's extensive trials with pulverised and colloidal fuels require to be examined. These have usually been explained as an attempt to combat the rising cost of coal caused by wartime inflation, and while the experiments certainly involved a much cheaper grade of fuel, it is strange that no other companies appear to have considered such economies at this time, despite the fact that there were few other railways which enjoyed the Great Central's advantage of somewhat lower fuel costs on account of its close proximity to the coalfields. From Robinson's point of view, the main advantage of these alternative fuels was that they involved mechanical feeding of the firebox. In a most exhaustive series of trials lasting from 1916 to 1924 four different 2-8-0s and a Glenalmond 4-6-0 were converted for varying periods of time to either pulverised or colloidal fuel. The fact that the experiments continued into the Grouping era is an indication of the importance which was attached to them, and although by this time Robinson was no longer in charge at Gorton it is interesting that for the first two years of LNER ownership he was retained by the new company as a consultant; similarly R. A. Thom, who had acted as Robinson's right hand man during the later stages of the trials, remained on the spot as LNER District Mechanical Engineer, Gorton to oversee the work.

The trials were abandoned in February 1924, and such meagre accounts as have been published suggest that they were not successful, but this does not appear to have been the view taken by certain important individuals. R. A. Thom, for example, claimed later on that they had been a success, while in 1928, R. H. Whitelegg, sometime Chief Mechanical Engineer of the GSWR and General Manager, Beyer Peacock 1921-1929, remarked during a discussion that 'the Grouping rather put an end to these developments'. So it may be that these schemes, like other experiments in progress at the time of Grouping, were abandoned simply because of lack of interest on the part of the new owners. However the trials had by this time acquired a special significance, for one of the last acts of the independent GCR was to place the order for the first two of its super-mineral engines.

In its final expiring effort to go ahead with the long-maturing plans, the company reverted back to the original idea of employing a Garratt. The reasons for this choice are not known, but it is interesting that at this time the ties between the GCR and Beyer Peacock & Co were about to be drawn considerably closer. With the termination of his duties as General Manager of the GC, Sir Sam Fay accepted a directorship of Peacock's and was promptly elected Chairman. In February 1924 Robinson also joined the Board. These two men would obviously have the keenest interest in the Garratt project especially the latter as it constituted in effect his last design for the old company; and this of course was in spite of the termination of the experiments with alternative fuels, which had occurred at the very same time that he became a director of Peacock's. Another member of the Peacock Board who would be likely to give support to any GC project was S. W. Pilling, who had formerly been a director of the Mansfield Railway. In the face of so much encouragement from the builders, and with the order already on the books, Gresley was thus faced with something approaching a fait accompli in his capacity as LNER Chief Mechanical Engineer.

Gresley's own attitude to the Garratt patent had been made clear in 1920, when he publicly declared that in Britain articulated locomotives were unnecessary. As though to prove the point, one of his earliest proposal to the Traffic Committee was for the construction of a conventional heavy mineral engine embodying the 2-8-2 wheel arrangement and later classed 'P1' by the LNER. Two examples were to be built at an estimated cost of £8,000 each, and approval for this was given by the Locomotive Committee on 2 August 1923; two days later the same Committee noted the intention to purchase two Garratts at a cost of approximately £10,000 each.

It is reasonable to assume that Gresley's attitude to the Garratt principle had not altered in any way since his elevation to the post of LNER Chief Mechanical Engineer, and so it is fairly certain that he would have been a good deal less enthusiastic about the ex-GC scheme than he was about the building of the two 'P1s'. So far as the former was concerned he was in all probability simply going along with the existing situation, and had he felt more established in his new position he might well have preferred to abandon the idea altogether. It is therefore not surprising that in the succeeding October we find the Garratt order being reduced to one engine only.

At about this time however a new factor entered into the proceedings. The LNER took the opportunity of buying from the government a large number of surplus 2-8-0s of the ex-GC '8K' type. These engines were bought extremely cheaply, and the company thus acquired a large fleet of heavy mineral locomotives at only a fraction of the true cost. The effect of this on the work of the CME's department is likely to have been felt in one of two ways. On the one hand, there would be little point in going ahead with the construction of new mineral engines, since the 2-8-0s would be capable of doing all that was required, and on the other, the money saved by the purchase of the 2-8-0s may have made the Board willing to sanction expenditure for experimental projects. The company were now being charged the sum of £14,395 for the solitary Garratt, and it seems unlikely that the Board would have accepted this expense on a purely experimental machine unless the circumstances had been favourable in some way, particularly as the CME himself was not really sold on the idea.

If this was indeed how Gresley felt, then his attitude and the subsequent suspension of the experiments with alternative fuels meant that the possibility of the Garratt being used in the manner intended by Robinson was waning steadily, if in fact it had not already disappeared altogether by the time the order was placed in April 1924. However, Gresley did retain enough interest in the project to propose in July that the engine should be altered to incorporate his favourite arrangement of three cylinders and conjugated valve gear, although this may have been nothing more than a move towards standardisation; and obviously, like all designers, he preferred to make use of his own patent whenever possible. The alteration was of significance in that it ran counter to the instructions originally issued by Peacock's, which stated that the overall weight of the engine was to be kept within very

specific limits; it also raised the tractive effort considerably beyond what had first been envisaged.

Whatever Gresley's thoughts as to the role the Garratt was destined to play, the railway press seemed to have few doubts; in July the influential magazine *Modern Transport* announced that it was the intention of the LNER 'to use the Garratt locomotives between Barnsley and Manchester on mineral traffic'. The reference to more than one Garratt suggests that the information had been obtained somewhat earlier and not checked subsequently; however the remark does imply that at this time the engine was still envisaged as going into main line service. However, in view of the fact that it was the first Garratt built for one of the British companies it seems surprising that there was not more speculation as to how it would be used, and the reasons why such a type was chosen. For the Woodhead service in particular the Garratt offered advantages which would have represented a marked improvement on previous types; the immense power of the machine would dispense with the use of banking engines on the heavy gradients, and on downhill sections the additional brake-power would be invaluable; the fact that the Garratts did not need to be turned would help to simplify the problem of engine movements at Gorton and Mexborough Locos, the two sheds which they would visit most frequently if used on the Woodhead service; and in the well-protected cab of the Garratt the crew would enjoy a greater degree of comfort. In addition, the use of Garratts would mean that the total number of engines employed on the mineral services could be reduced, and fewer crews required; and also it would have been possible to speed up the mineral trains somewhat, on account of the extra power and braking capacity. To achieve all these gains a fleet of Garratts would have been required, and no doubt this was Robinson's intention, subject to the first two having proved satisfactory. If such a scheme was ever discussed seriously by the LNER, it is unlikely to have been received with enthusiasm on account of the high cost; the purchase of Class 8K 2-8-0s from the Government has already been mentioned, these being engines which had long since proved themselves highly suitable for the mineral services, and by 1925 further examples were on offer at the absurdly low price of £1,500 each. As has already been remarked, this alone made the building of new mineral engines an unnecessarily expensive course. The ultimate demise of the Garratt as a main line engine may therefore have been due mainly to financial policy rather than to any objections on Gresley's part, and this may also be the underlying reason for the abandonment of the fuel experiments.

It is interesting that when the LMS turned their attention to the possibilities of the Garratt type they followed a similar course to that which, it is suggested, would have been adopted by Robinson had not his scheme been overtaken by Grouping. They built a fleet of Garratts for use on a specific mineral service, and so were able to reap most if not all of the advantages outlined above. Such basic difficulties as they did encounter lay in the design of bunker, and shortcomings in the general performance seem to have been traceable to the existence of certain

Midland Railway features in their design. The LNER engine would, hopefully, have been free of such faults.

The machine was delivered to Gorton on Sunday 21 June 1925. We can imagine a knot of curious officials congregating round it, among them almost certainly W. G. P. Maclure, who was in the habit of visiting Gorton regularly on Sundays at this time, and whose responsibility it would ultimately be to decide on the work to be performed by this monster. He more than anybody would have been aware of the extent to which the likely role of the Garratt had altered now that it was dependent on hand-firing. A test took place on the same day, with the engine working on the main line as far as Woodhead or possibly beyond, but as the train consisted of only two passenger coaches — presumably conveying various officers and staff — the run was evidently not a test in the true sense of the word; with the Garratt still in shop grey, the ensemble must have seemed a very curious apparition to those lucky enough to catch sight of it. Short as the run was however, it is highly likely that the actual difficulties of firing the Garratt were fully realised by the time it was over; in a short report appearing next day in the *Daily Dispatch* there was reference to 'a giant engine burning $2\frac{1}{2}$ tons of coal an hour'. A piece of journalistic licence, no doubt, but nonetheless an indication of the sort of problems that had arisen.

Within a couple of days the machine was back inside Peacock's, where some detail alterations were rather hastily made. Here we need to take note of yet another complication in the already very chequered history of the Garratt, for it had been arranged that it should take part in the Railway Centenary Exhibition, which was due to open at Darlington in a few days' time; for some reason it was deemed necessary for these adjustments to be made prior to its appearance at the Centenary, and they were completed by the contractors in the space of about three days. They included provision of vent-pipes to the water tanks, vertical handrails on the front footplating, and replacement of the original round buffers by oval ones of a pattern similar to those fitted by the GCR to some of its larger engines. Brackets were also fitted to the coal-bunker to take the fire-irons, and as these obscured the letters 'LNER' painted high up on the bunker side the letters and numbers were repositioned. The former were painted centrally on the frames below the boiler, and the numbers were repainted on the front tank and bunker, but were now a good deal larger and spaced noticeably further apart; they were in fact larger than the LNER standard, and possibly this was intended as a kind of 'exhibition finish'. The engine remained in workshop grey however, presumably because there was not enough time to take it across to Gorton for the final finish to be applied.

The machine left Gorton on Friday 26 June, with Driver Jack Hopley at the regulator for the initial stage of the run; the indefatigable *Daily Dispatch* published a photograph of it passing Woodhead station, travelling chimney-first as it had done on the trial of the previous Sunday. According to *Locomotives of the LNER* Part 9B, it was bound for Doncaster, where it underwent a trial run

to Retford and back before being finally despatched to Darlington. No official details of this run appear to have survived.

Precisely what kind of plans had been made for the Garratt at the time of its appearance at the Centenary is difficult to determine. Almost certainly, by this stage, the decision had been taken that it would be used as a banker at Worsborough; an article published in the *Railway Gazette* a few days before it left Manchester stated that it would be used as a banker on the Worsborough line, and this was echoed in the magazine *Engineering* when an issue appearing on the day the engine departed carried the announcement that it was 'intended for banking work on the steepest gradients of the system'. However there is nothing in the official LNER literature dealing with the Exhibition, and perhaps the company were not particularly anxious to advertise the fact that their largest and most expensive piece of hardware was to be used in such a humble role.

It is strange however that at this stage the Garratt still retained its vacuum brake connections at front and rear. If the engine was to work as a banker these were virtually useless, and could well have been removed during its visit to Beyer Peacock's if the decision had in fact been taken at that stage. It is equally curious that they still remained in position after a visit to Doncaster Works following the exhibition appearance. Their retention suggests that the Loco Running Department were still casting round for some main line role which the engine could fulfil, and there are reports of it having worked trains from Dewsnap Yard to Wath, and also from Wath to Immingham, but these have not been confirmed, and there is nothing to indicate that any sort of official tests were ever carried out. In view of the revolutionary nature of the engine this is surprising; the only explanation seems to be that the management completely lost interest in it once it had dropped out of the limelight after the Centenary, and that it then quietly took up its duties at Worsborough, though still retaining its vacuum pipes as a kind of symbol of the better things it might have achieved.

During its visit to Doncaster it was repainted in the LNER black livery then applied to goods engines, which included red lining-out, and the large exhibition numerals were replaced by others conforming more closely to LNER standard. It was in this guise that it took up work at Worsborough, although the precise date of that event is not known.

Officially allocated to Mexborough, the Garratt operated from Wentworth, which was classed as an outstation of Mexborough although geographically nearer to the shed at Barnsley. This spot, for it can hardly be described as a shed, was part-way up the Worsborough branch gradient, a short distance before the steepest part of the climb began. The pattern of working revolved round what were known as 'double-loads', these being trains of approximately 63 wagons containing altogether about 1,000 tons of coal; 'single-loads' of about half this size and weight went up the bank unassisted by the banker. A 'double-load' started out from Wath Yard with two Class 8K 2-8-0 engines at the head and proceeded as far as Wombwell, where a stop was made during which the leading engine transferred to the rear for the first stage of the assault on the bank; several miles of steady climbing now ensued until Wentworth was reached, and here the train halted again to allow the Garratt to join on behind the rear engine. The whole procession then ascended the last $2\frac{1}{2}$ miles on a gradient of 1 in 40 to rejoin the Barnsley-Penistone main line at West Silkstone Junction. Towards the summit of the climb there were two short tunnels, and with the passage of three engines working full out the atmosphere inside these can be better imagined than described. The average time for the climb from Wentworth was about 13min, but this could be considerably improved upon by keen crews and the record stood at 8min. Having reached West Silkstone the Garratt dropped off and ran back light down the gradient to await its next customer. In a 24-hour spell the engine was expected to be able to bank 18 trains during times of busy traffic, but in practice the average was about 13. It remained at Wentworth all through the working week and went to Mexborough Loco on Sunday mornings for routine maintenance.

Responsibility for manning the Garratt was shared between Mexborough and Barnsley crews, with the former being out-stationed at Wentworth and the Barnsley men travelling; the latter also covered any absences. With round-the-clock working, three shifts were required.

The Garratt received an extremely cool reception from the footplatemen. The crews who worked on the Worsborough line had long been accustomed to the GCR eight-coupled types, which they regarded as outstanding for the work, and as at Gorton they were very anti-GN, having formed a poor opinion of the engines built by that company. The knowledge that the Garratt had been designed by Gresley was enough to prejudice them from the start. Another very important factor was the influence of the unions. Following the successful strike of 1919 the railway unions, along with others, were flexing their muscles, and the men were increasingly on the look-out for what were considered to be abuses. The Garratt was seen as a means by which the work of two crews could be done by one, and this was strongly resented, especially at a time when the country was already settling into the interwar slump; no doubt there were particularly vociferous complaints from the firemen, who were expected to fire a grate twice the size of that they had been used to on the '8Ks', or 'O4s' as they were now called.

Even apart from these prejudices however, the Garratt was soon found to have serious limitations as a banking engine. One of the most difficult problems was visibility; in order to keep the maximum depth of water over the firebox crown the engine was worked chimney-first, which meant that because of the leading tank the driver was too far back to be able to judge distances properly when approaching the rear of a train to commence banking; his vision was further restricted by the escape of steam from the flexible joints, a problem aggravated by the usually cool rural air. Difficulties of vision were compounded by other handicaps; when the engine was standing the brake

cylinders quickly cooled, and steam admitted to the pipes tended to condense when work was resumed, interfering with braking efficiency, and as if this was not enough the regulator was extremely stiff, requiring a pull of 60lb to open it, according to *Locomotives of the LNER*. For all these reasons very great care had therefore to be exercised when the engine was coming up to the rear of a train, especially when contact was to be made with a brake-van. Not surprisingly a number of minor collisions are understood to have occurred, and there were many guards who preferred to descend and stand to one side when the Garratt was joining on at the rear. During the climb the engine was capable of lifting wagons bodily into the air if the regulator was carelessly handled, such was the power. As for the fireman, although he was able to rest for quite long periods, he had an onerous task once the banking began, and his burdens were added to by the necessity to get coal forward from the back of the bunker after a few trips. Both members of the crew had the worst of the atmospheric conditions in the tunnels as the Garratt was invariably the last to pass through; as recounted in *Locomotives of the LNER*, some experiments were made with respirators but they were not successful. The very fact that respirators were provided however gives some indication of how severe the conditions were.

Garratt duty rapidly became the most unpopular turn at the sheds involved, and dislike of the engine reached such a pitch that a deliberate ruse was adopted to put it out of action. This consisted of closing the dampers and then putting on the injectors, a manoeuvre which caused the tubes to begin leaking. The engine then had to return to Mexborough for attention, and two stand-by 'O4s' were then sent in its place. The frequency of these 'failures' drew official attention, and during the course of an investigation by Inspector Dixon of Doncaster the trick was discovered; strict instructions were then issued to the effect that there must be no recurrence.

Ability to manoeuvre the Garratt seems to have improved slightly as the men accumulated experience, but the passage of time revealed a further serious headache. The water supply at both Wentworth and Mexborough was as bad as any on the entire GC system, and the Garratt soon fell a victim to it. By the end of July 1926, only 12 months after first going into service, it was in Doncaster Works for retubing, and within another 12 months was back yet again, requiring repair to a cracked firebox tubeplate; the lack of a spare boiler meant that the engine was out of service during these repairs, the total absence on these two occasions being over five months. If any evidence is needed to show that the employment of the Garratt at Worsborough was an unplanned manoeuvre, this is surely it; the GC management had long been well aware of the water situation in the locality, and would not have been likely to allow an engine to be regularly based there without the prospect of transfer to another district to extend the period between repairs.

The LNER tackled the problem by treatment of the water. A supply of the necessary chemical was carried on board the locomotive in the form of large solids about the size of a football, and the crew were responsible for depositing one of these in the tank at each filling. At the start this brought an improvement in repair mileages, probably because of official supervision in the early stages of treating the water, but performance tailed off again later as the men apparently forgot to add the chemicals from time to time, or as sometimes happened, threw them into a convenient ditch.

Even after treatment the water was still bad, as was well known even before Grouping, and in consequence the Garratt's availability record was extremely poor. In the 14 years up to 1939 it made 16 recorded visits to Doncaster Works, being out of service for a total of three years altogether. This does not include time spent out of service while awaiting repair, nor the innumerable visits to Mexborough Loco for minor attention. The average mileage between repairs was just under 24,000.

For much of 1926 the Garratt had little work to do because of the coal strike, which began at the same time as the General Strike in May and lasted for the rest of the year. During this period the engine was officially booked to work from 6.00am Monday to 9.00pm Saturday, but as almost all the traffic on the Worsborough Branch was coal it would have had very little employment.

Because of its status as the most powerful engine in the country, the Garratt came to be much in demand for the rolling stock exhibitions which the LNER frequently staged during the thirties. Its first known appearance in one of these was on Monday 31 March 1930 when a display of goods locomotives and vehicles was staged at Sheffield Victoria in conjunction with the local Rotary Club; the Garratt hauled a train of assorted goods wagons from Doncaster to Sheffield, with the Lord Mayor of Sheffield riding on the footplate for part of the way. After the show was over the Garratt left for Doncaster Works, to spend eight months there having a new firebox fitted. The exhibitions usually occupied a weekend, as for example the one held at Doncaster Works on 26 and 27 May 1934, when the Garratt appeared in the company of such engines as No 4472 *Flying Scotsman*, No 2832 *Belvoir Castle*, and the new No 2001 *Cock o' the North*. These weekend appearances suggest that its presence at Worsborough was hardly deemed essential.

From a financial point of view the Garratt must have represented a singularly poor investment. The excessive first cost of the machine, together with the ever-growing repair bill, would have shown up in a poor light when compared with the cost of the alternative, which was to make use of two 'O4s'. The LMS, on the other hand, enjoyed the advantages of buying in quantity; once their first fleet of 33 Garratts had got into their stride on the Toton-Brent coal trains the company President, Sir Josiah Stamp, was able to claim a saving of one set of men per train with the elimination of double-heading, and the displacement of 68 freight engines, not to mention increased speed of the trains and an approximate saving of 15% in coal. The LNER, alas, could not even claim a saving in men, as because of the frequent failures, a spare crew had to be kept on hand at Barnsley. And yet, ironically, the LNER Garratt is thought to have been the better design of the two. Its shortcomings at Worsborough should not be allowed to blind us to its possibilities as a main line machine; working alongside others of its type, benefiting from a properly varied water supply, and mechanically fired either by Robinson's methods or by some other, it may well have achieved a revolution as a heavy mineral engine. A fair verdict would seem to be that it was an excellent idea given the wrong application.

Perhaps the possibilities of the engine can be still better seen when it is remembered that Robinson's original conception was based on the Class 8K 2-8-0, probably the best locomotive he ever designed. Had the machine appeared in this form it is likely that it would have been largely standard with the '8K' in respect of controls and other features. Thus it would not have had to overcome the prejudice which greeted the Gresley variant, and on main line work it may well have been found to possess the excellent '8K' characteristics. If so it would have been a remarkable engine indeed.

97
In public view for the first time on Sunday 21 June 1925, the Garratt is seen from the Audenshaw Road overbridge near Fairfield as it makes its first trial trip up to Woodhead. The letters 'LNER' on the tank top will be noted.
W. H. Whitworth courtesy H. C. Casserley

98
The Garratt back in Peacock's work after its first trials. The letters on the front tank have been obliterated with black paint.
North Western Museum of Science & Industry

99
The Garratt, as repainted with large numerals for the Railway Centenary Exhibition, seen in Peacock's works yard.
Real Photographs

100
The Garratt as Exhibit No 42 at the Railway Centenary, 1925. In 1923-4 both Sir Sam Fay and John G. Robinson were still on the LNER payroll, as well as being directors of Beyer Peacock's. In 1924 James Hadfield, a young draughtsman from the GC Gorton drawing office also joined Beyer Peacocks and eventually rose to the position of Chairman. *Real Photographs*

99

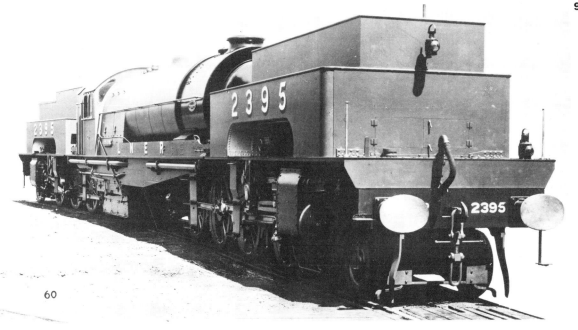

60

100

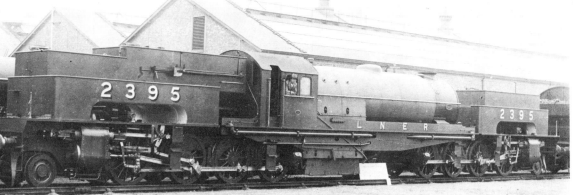

101
In 1921 No 966 converted to burn oil fuel as part of the extensive trials undertaken by John G. Robinson. *Real Photographs*

102
At the Sheffield Rotary Club Exhibition, 30 March 1930. *North Western Museum of Science & Industry*

103
Mexborough Loco, April 1939. The Garratt is alongside the electric turntable.   *W. Potter*

104
Away from the Worsborough bank the Garratt was usually to be found inside Doncaster Works. This view was taken outside the paint shop in April 1938 after the engine had undergone a general repair.   *W. Potter*

104

105
An all-too-familiar spectacle at Mexborough Loco. The Garratt is out of use, and the sign above the buffer beam reads 'Not to Be Moved — Engine Disabled'.
F. Elliott/Authors' Collection

106
One of the few views of the Garratt at work on the Worsborough Bank. The date is 23 April 1947 and the engine has been renumbered. *H. C. Casserley*

107
'O4' No 6250 pictured about 1930 climbing towards the Silkstone tunnels on the Worsborough branch with a westbound coal train.
R. H. N. Clay/Rail Archive Stephenson

108
'O4s' Nos 6208 and 6254 bank a coal train towards the Silkstone tunnels, Worsborough branch, 1930.
R. H. N Clay/Rail Archive Stephenson

11
Highdyke-Frodingham Ironstone Trains

The origins of the traffic between Highdyke, a short distance from Grantham on the GN main line, and the great iron and steel centre of Frodingham go back to pre-Grouping days. In 1916 the Frodingham Iron & Steel Company, working in conjunction with the Appleby Iron Company, carried out their first survey of the Northamptonshire sands ironstone bed in the area round Colsterworth, some miles south of Grantham. At that time the Frodingham blast furnaces relied heavily on locally mined ore, which despite being relatively poor in quality was to be found in abundance, and possessed the advantages that it was easily won and contained enough limestone to make the charge self-fluxing. However, even as early as 1874 it had been realised that the furnaces operated more easily and economically if a proportion of siliceous ore was included in the charge, and agreements had been made with the Mid-Lincolnshire Ironstone Company to obtain ore of this kind from their mines at Greetwell, a short distance east of Lincoln on the then MSLR Lincoln-Barnetby line. Over the years the resources of these began to give out, and with the increasing demands on the iron and steel industry brought about by the armament programme before and during the Great War, consideration of an alternative source became necessary. The trials with Colsterworth ore proved successful, and as there was already a branch line in existence connecting Stainby, in the heart of the ironstone area, with the GNR main line at Highdyke, just south of Grantham, the Frodingham and Appleby Companies were able to begin operations at once. The branch had been built in 1915 as a result of proposals put forward by another concern, the Holwell Iron Company, but as their operations were conducted only on a modest scale it was the traffic of the two larger companies which quickly formed the bulk of the tonnage worked on the branch. Not long after they became interested in the Highdyke branch, the Frodingham and Appleby Companies were amalgamated in a new organisation called United Steel, and in 1934 they became jointly known as the Appleby-Frodingham Steel Company.

A Working Timetable dated August 1919 gives the branch as in operation except that certain sidings were shown as not yet in use. A timetable of October 1922 shows full operation, although neither on this nor the earlier one are any actual trains given, these being worked 'as required'.

No sooner had the branch got into full swing than the postwar boom came to an end, and the depression in trade was faithfully reflected in the fortunes of the Colsterworth developments during the 1920s. However the United Steel Co had a definite commitment to increase steel-making at the Frodingham and Appleby furnaces and from 1926, notwithstanding the General Strike and

coal strike that followed, a decided improvement took place; two new mines, Colsterworth No 2 and Colsterworth Glebe, were opened, and were eventually followed by Colsterworth No 2 Extension, Cringle Pit and Cringle Pit Extension, opened during the 1930s. Despite the continuing decline of the iron industry in other areas during these years, therefore, the Colsterworth area entered its most prosperous period up to that time. Nor did the United Steel Co have anything approaching a monopoly of the branch, for supplies of ironstone were sent to the Stanton Iron Co, and the branch also served Sproxton, where there was an ironstone mine owned by the Parkgate Iron & Steel Company of Rotherham.

With expanding production the branch required the services of two regular engines, busy hauling empty wagons to the various mines and bringing back loaded vehicles to the sidings specially provided at Highdyke. A Working Timetable for 1931 shows the first engine booked off Grantham Loco at 7am, and the second 45min later. Before proceeding on to the branch the latter collected empties at Grantham as necessary. Between 8.10am and 8.20pm there were 13 trips timetabled on the branch, each consisting of empties to the mines and loaded wagons on the return, the engines returning to Grantham Loco after the last return journey. Most trains were worked to and from Stainby, which was just under six miles from the branch junction at Highdyke, but several continued to Sproxton, another two miles further on. The branch was single-line throughout, and was worked by electric tablet as far as Skillington Road, which was an approximate mid-point of the line, and then by train staff beyond.

After dropping to 11 trips each way in 1935, perhaps as a result of the depression of the years immediately before, the branch service had risen to 15 trips by 1938. The rise may well have been a reflection of increased trade as a result of rearmament.

Work on the branch was performed by a variety of locomotive types. The indigenous 0-6-0s of Classes J3 and J6 were used initially, but in the mid-1930s two strangers came on the scene in the shape of ex-GE 'J15' 0-6-0s Nos 7515 and 7696. These latter two were stationed at Grantham from February 1936 until the following April, and it may be inferred from this short stay that they were not a success. Further visitors arrived the following year, this time from the NE Area; they were Class J21 No 1806, which came in May, and No 26 in the succeeding August. Both had gone by the end of 1938, and so were presumably not much of an improvement on the former GE engines. It seems fairly certain that the reason behind these manoeuvres was the increasing traffic on the branch; in the late 1930s the output of the Appleby-Frodingham Co's mines had climbed to 700,000 tons per annum from an average of only 400,000 in the previous decade, and in all probability attempts were being made to work heavier trains. The use of more modern wagons of greater capacity may also have played a part. The branch was steeply graded in both directions, and the work had been difficult enough even in the earlier years. The problem was made worse by the fact that only certain engine types were permitted.

Grantham was host to a miscellany of 0-6-0 tank engine types throughout the 1930s, and it is possible that some of these may have been tried on the Highdyke trips. They included Class J66 and J69 engines from the GE Section, a 'J77' from the NE Area, and also a GC 'N5' from Sheffield; the last named, No 5761, came for a few months in the spring of 1932. It is doubtful if any of these various classes of engine was employed on the branch for any length of time, although all may well have been tried out. There has also been a suggestion that a former Hull & Barnsley 0-6-0 tender engine was used for a time, but this has not been confirmed.

So far as the main line trains were concerned, they were originally routed directly along the GN main line as far as Doncaster, where they diverged on to the GC Doncaster-Grimsby route. Grantham engines and men worked as far as Doncaster Mineral Sidings, where they handed over to GC engines and men from Keadby Loco, a shed destined to be replaced by a more modern establishment at Frodingham in 1932. At the beginning of 1928 this working was booked to leave Highdyke at 1.10pm and reached the Mineral Sidings at 7.8, but later in the year this section of the trip was greatly speeded up, with departure from Highdyke at 1.20pm and arrival in Doncaster more than $1\frac{1}{2}$ hours earlier at 5.35. During this year the programme for improvements at the Frodingham end began to take effect, with a brand new yard being opened to receive the ironstone trains.

The steadily growing volume of work which the ironstone traffic generated had a considerable effect on life at Grantham, furnishing additional employment and offering improved promotion prospects at a time when the reverse was the order of the day everywhere else. By 1931, a time when the slump was hitting railway traffics badly, there were two daily trains to Frodingham, and the fact that the 1.20pm was now taking more than an hour longer suggests that it had increased in weight; such things were in marked contrast to the general trend at that time.

At some date in the period 1932-3 a major change of route was made. Instead of going via Doncaster, the ironstone trains were now turned off the GN main line at Barkston South, proceeded via Honington and Leadenham to Lincoln where they joined the GC Lincoln-Grimsby line, with a final reversal at Barnetby for the short haul into Frodingham. The switch was influenced by several powerful factors, of which the most important was probably the general acceleration of traffic on the GN main line in the spring of 1932; it was clearly an operating advantage to remove the slow-moving ironstone trains. A further bonus was that on the lightly-occupied Grantham-Lincoln and Lincoln-Barnetby lines they would be subject to a good deal less delay, while at the

Frodingham end the opening of the new loco shed meant that these facilities were now handily adjacent to the local yards, thus reducing light engine running. Yet another gain was that the two separate engine workings which had been operated on the original Doncaster route were condensed to one, with the same locomotive and men doing the whole trip.

This recasting of the service was thus highly advantageous, and the only drawback lay in the rather complicated movements necessary to negotiate the passage of Lincoln. As is the case in any locality where a number of routes converge at street level, the city was a cat's cradle of junctions and level crossings, each a major obstacle because of conflicting traffic movements, and the absence of an avoiding line meant that the ironstone trains had to be threaded through in a most tortuous manner. Entering the city precincts at Sincil Junction, the train was now travelling in the wrong direction, and in order to reverse had to reach the goods road between East Holmes and West Holmes signalboxes; this involved traversing the infamous Durham Ox level-crossing, running through the passenger station, negotiating a second level crossing over High Street, a third at Brayford, and then crossing a swing-bridge before at last the train could be drawn clear of the running lines. The engine uncoupled and ran forward for about a mile to turn on the turntable at Pyewipe Junction, once the property of the GER, and then came back to be attached at the other end of its train. In the meantime the guard also changed ends, the ironstone trains being invariably provided with a brake-van at each end for this purpose, and the train then set off to retrace its obstacle-strewn course to the Durham Ox crossing in order to reach the Grimsby line. The continual stopping and starting which this manoeuvre involved would have been bad enough even for a light-weight train, and the lumbering load of ironstone, loose-coupled throughout, must have made agonisingly slow progress. And it sometimes happened that it was not possible to reverse the train in this way because of occupation of the goods road at West Holmes, in which event an even more complicated manoeuvre had to be resorted to whereby the engine propelled its train through a triangular movement, West Holmes-Pyewipe-Boultham Junction-West Holmes, so as to finish up facing in the right direction.

On both sides of Lincoln the train passed through territory which coincidentally held many associations with the ironstone industry. Near Honington Junction, a few miles north of Grantham, were defunct quarries once belonging to the Stanton Iron Co, and the same ironstone field was traversed a little further north at Caythorpe, where the once-extensive workings were spread at either side of the station; a certain amount of ironstone mining was still carried on here, with GN 0-6-0s and Grantham-based Sentinel engines working the railway traffic during the early 1930s. At Leadenham, the next station north, siliceous ironstone had once been mined and forwarded to one of the United Steel's neighbours at Frodingham, John Lysaght's of Normanby Park. North of Lincoln the ironstone trains passed the once-prosperous mines at

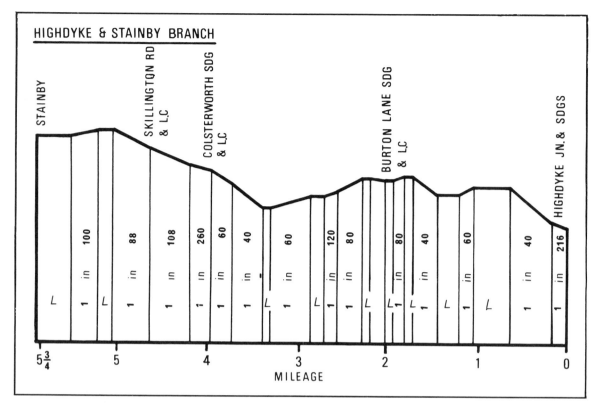

HIGHDYKE & STAINBY BRANCH

Fig 2
Gradient profile of the Highdyke branch.

Greetwell, which had supplied the Frodingham furnaces with siliceous ore for so many years; ancient, derelict mines were present about 15 miles further on at Claxby, and not far from there lay John Lysaght's sidings, where the aerial ropeway adjacent to Holton-le-Moor station betrayed underground workings high in the Lincolnshire Wolds.

Arrival at Barnetby, some nine miles east of Frodingham, meant a second reversal of the train. Here a turntable was conveniently situated at the lineside, but drivers of the ironstone trains preferred to ignore it, and simply ran round their trains to work the remaining short distance tender-first; this considerably expedited the manoeuvre, and as a banking pilot was waiting to assist the train forward as far as Santon, in the immediate vicinity of Frodingham, this final stage of the journey was accomplished relatively quickly. From Santon the engine had only to take its train a short distance forward to North Lincoln Junction, where the steelworks line left the GC Doncaster-Grimsby route, and it was then released to run light to Frodingham Loco. The train was broken up and the wagons taken forward in batches to whichever works required them.

Empty trains followed exactly the same route in reverse, including reversal at Barnetby and the long-drawn-out series of manoeuvres in Lincoln; the only material difference was that the empties started from Frodingham New Yard, a spacious network of sidings adjacent to the passenger station and further west than North Lincoln Junction. Here the pilots brought the empty ironstone wagons back from the works, marshalling them alongside trains of newly-produced steel. Both empty and loaded ironstone trains ran as Class C and on an average took about six hours to complete the journey, though there were considerable variations.

With the change in route a guaranteed service was introduced consisting of two loaded trains daily, this being sufficient for the needs of the United Steel Co's blast furnaces in Frodingham.

It was not the company's practice to maintain large stocks of ore, as in common with most other industrial enterprises at that period they operated with tightly-drawn purse strings. Of the two trains, the faithful 1.20pm ex-Highdyke was still running at this time, followed by another departure at 4.35pm.

From the start the rerouted service was run on a lodging basis, shared between Frodingham and Grantham men. Though not exactly an innovation at Grantham, lodging there was something out of the ordinary, and since Grouping little work of this kind had been done, as was the case with most GN Section sheds. The Frodingham men, by contrast, were veteran lodgers in the best GC tradition, and Grantham was merely another name on the long list of places where they were accustomed to lay their heads. Frodingham men known to have worked to Grantham in the period up to 1939 include Fred

Morris, Tommy Allan, Harry Oldfield, Bill Jewitt and Mark Tingle, while among the Grantham men there were Harry Royce, Arthur Goodson, Harold Winch, Charlie Clayton, Percy Braybrook, Arthur Measures and Bob Dodd. No doubt a number of the latter became familiar faces at Kings Cross when they eventually progressed to the Grantham Top Link in later years.

As timetabled, the ironstone trains fitted conveniently into an eight-hour shift, and may even have allowed for engine disposal on completion of the trip; however the possibility of delay, particularly at Lincoln, would no doubt have made arrival times rather variable. At July 1935 the same basic service was still operating, although the times were now somewhat different. The former 4.35pm departure from Highdyke had given way to a completely new train leaving at 3.55 in the morning, and the long-standing 1.20pm had been retimed to leave 5min earlier. Empty trains left Frodingham at 5.10am and 12.30pm, the turns no doubt being arranged so that the former was worked by the men who had reached Frodingham the previous day with the early morning departure from Highdyke, which got in at 9.25am. The average time spent off duty at both ends was about 16 hours, quite a sizeable allowance for a lodging turn.

At Frodingham the engines for both empty trains were booked to come off the shed 35min before departure time, this a generous allowance in view of the short distance to the New Yard. Departure times of locomotives coming off Grantham shed have not been traced, but the engine for the 3.55am was booked to pass Grantham passenger station, a short distance from the Loco, at 3.15, and the engine of the second train came past at 12.5pm, a full hour and 10min before eventual departure. This engine was taken out by the crew booked to work the second shift on the Highdyke Pilot; they relieved the first shift crew at Highdyke, these men then working the 1.15pm train as far as Grantham station, where the main line men took over. Light engine mileage was considerably greater at the Grantham end than at Frodingham, as Highdyke was four miles south of Grantham station.

The increase in the Highdyke branch services in the late 1930s, mentioned earlier, was reflected in a more frequent main line service; by 1938 a 9.50pm departure from Highdyke had been added, running as required, and in 1939 the departures numbered no fewer than four. Besides the two regulars there were trains at 10am and 4.20pm, the latter running as required. Balancing turns from Frodingham comprised the original 5.10am and 12.30pm, together with others at 11.20am and 5pm, although the 12.30pm had been demoted to run as required. To even up the workings, it was arranged that when the 4.20pm ex-Highdyke was running, its crew should change over with the men on the 5pm from Frodingham; the change was made at Market Rasen and applied also to guards. Another empty train which ran for a spell during this period left Frodingham at 1.15pm, and somewhat curiously the engine was diagrammed to come off at Grantham Station, instead of going through to Highdyke as did all the others.

Such developments indicate that business was booming, and by this period other concerns in addition to the Appleby-Frodingham Co were involved in the traffic. These included John Lysaght's and Richard Thomas, and the wider variety of destinations raised marshalling problems, even though all the firms were based at Frodingham. There was insufficient siding capacity at Highdyke to assemble the trains in proper sequence, so that they arrived rough at Frodingham, but as far as possible the system was for the Appleby-Frodingham and Richard Thomas traffic to be detached at North Lincoln Junction, while that for Lysaght's was taken to another siding known as Yard No 2. There was also another Appleby-Frodingham works for which traffic had to be brought to a separate part of Yard No 2. The splitting-up of trains led to an exceptional amount of shunting and caused congestion at North Lincoln, but was improved to some extent by administrative measures involving closer co-operation between the Frodingham Yardmasters, which resulted in a cutting-down of conflicting traffic movements and better utilisation of pilot engines.

The ironstone trains were regularly worked by the standard weight-shifters of the GC Section, the Class O4 'Tinies'. Though the Lincolnshire gradients were a good deal less severe than those over Woodhead, the 2-8-0s had their work cut out with the trains of 65 loaded wagons which became the standard formation in the 1930s. The class had of course been familiar in North Lincolnshire ever since the first examples had been built at Gorton in the days before World War 1, but at Grantham they were strangers, and the posting of No 6634 in November 1928 must have been an event of some importance there, the engine doubtless attracting a great deal of attention from curious footplatemen. Alas, no record of their initial impressions has survived, but there is no doubt that in later years the class became very popular with the crews of the ironstone trains. The pioneer engine was one of those purchased from the Government by the LNER, and had been put into traffic at Gorton only five months before its arrival at Grantham. This series of engines were known as the 'ROD' class, and as the number of 'Tinies' at Grantham increased during the 1930s there came to be a heavy preponderance of the ex-Government type, these being readily distinguishable by their numbers in the 65XX and 66XX series. No 6634 was replaced by No 6604 in January 1931, and after that the allocation gradually expanded with the arrival of No 6535 in February 1933 and No 6635 in December 1935. During this period Nos 6321, 6606 and 6509 also had short spells at Grantham. The boom of the late 1930s was reflected in the arrival of Nos 6627/8 in May 1937, and by the outbreak of war the allocation had reached seven, comprising Nos 6244, 6533/5, 6604, 6627, 6628 and 6635.

Visiting Grantham Loco on Sunday 10 October 1937, an observer noted no fewer than seven engines of the 'O4' class; these were Nos 6535, 6604, 6627/35, all of Grantham, Nos 6191 and 6223 of Frodingham, and No 6595 of Doncaster. Thus was a flourishing GC atmosphere apparent in this GN stronghold.

The Class O4 engines were well represented at Frodingham, as at most major GC sheds; at the time of its opening in June 1932 there were 16 there all told, mostly 'ROD' engines. By the summer of 1939 expanding steel production had had its effect, causing the allocation to soar to 31, with other engines following directly after the outbreak of war; it should of course be remembered, however, that not all of these would be used on the iron-stone trains, as they covered a variety of other services besides. On the morning of Sunday 1 August 1937 a total of 15 'O4s' was noted on Frodingham Loco, including No 6628 of Grantham.

At an early stage the 'O4s' were tried on the Highdyke branch itself, but following derailments at Colsterworth and Stainby, caused by their lengthy wheelbase, they were barred. The problem of finding a suitable engine for the branch is one that does not seem to have been solved, or at least not before World War 2. Apart from the abortive attempt to use them in this role, the 'O4s' gave every satisfaction on the ironstone trains and as far as is known they monopolised them completely in the period under review.

The wagons which comprised these trains are known to have been of a modern all-metal hopper type, though probably not as large as similar vehicles in use elsewhere. The LNER are understood to have bought privately-built hopper wagons of no less than 25 tons capacity as early as 1926, but it is believed that those used on the Highdyke services were of a smaller variety, probably about 17 tons capacity. The existence of a regular balancing service of empties indicates that the wagons were restricted to the ironstone trains, and not allowed to be used on other services. However in addition to the Frodingham workings the pool of hoppers would probably cover the Parkgate trains referred to earlier, and perhaps also the lighter trains working between Frodingham and the Lysaght ironstone holdings at Holton-le-Moor. Considerable numbers of new hopper wagons were built from about 1936, no doubt as a result of the notably increasing traffic, and many of these vehicles would certainly have been allocated to Highdyke services.

The Highdyke-Frodingham trains are a typical example of a specialised mineral service of the interwar era, and from the time of re-routing were a familiar sight on a somewhat little-known part of the GC Section. The increase in the traffic is an indication of developments on a national level, and its growing importance in the LNER scheme of things may be judged from the fact that at one period consideration was given to plans for building by-pass lines both at Lincoln and Barnetby to simplify the working. However, like so many other projects in which the LNER was interested, the scheme fell through.

109
The Appleby-Frodingham and Redbourn iron and steel works photographed from about 1,500ft. This is a 1948 view, but it faithfully depicts the prewar destination of the Highdyke ironstone. The main line can be seen snaking across the top right-hand corner, and Frodingham Loco, identified by the white mark, is north of this. Between the wars this was the largest iron and steel-making complex in the British Empire. *BSC, Scunthorpe Division*

111

Loading ironstone in the Frodingham area in the 1930s. The work was much the same as that carried on at the Highdyke branch mines, with a huge mechanical excavator removing the overburden while small steam shovels load the ironstone into wagons. An Avonside tank engine heads a mixed train of private and assorted railway-owned wagons.
Scunthorpe Museum and and Art Gallery

Ironstone on the GC main line. An unidentified 'Tiny' between Ruddington and Nottingham, bound for Rotherham with a load of stone from the Parkgate Company's mines at Charwelton. *Real Photographs*

110

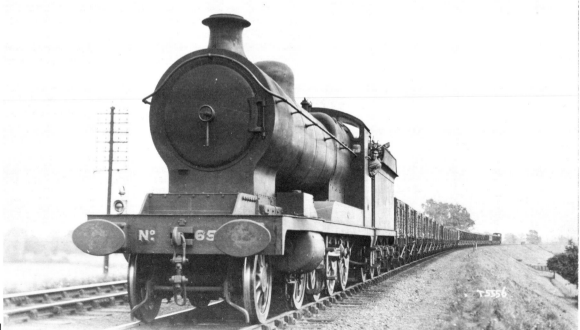

111

112
An unidentified 'O4' nears Grantham station with the 4.20pm Highdyke-Stanton ironstone train about 1930.
T. G. Hepburn/Rail Archive Stephenson

113
Class D3 No 4316, a visitor to the area, climbs away from Grantham past Saltersford with ironstone empties for Highdyke. The wagons are a mixture of Appleby Iron Company and Frodingham Iron & Steel Company hoppers
T. G. Hepburn/Rail Archive Stephenson

FRODINGHAM WORKS, SCUNTHORPE

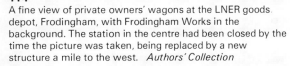

114
A fine view of private owners' wagons at the LNER goods
depot, Frodingham, with Frodingham Works in the
background. The station in the centre had been closed by the
time the picture was taken, being replaced by a new
structure a mile to the west. *Authors' Collection*

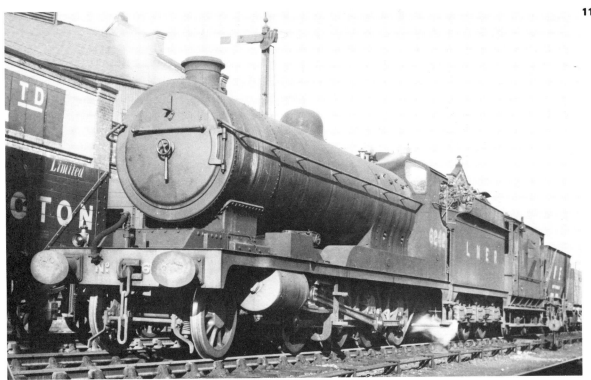

115
A rare shot of the Frodingham-Highdyke service in prewar days. 'O4' No 6242 of Frodingham passes the Ruston works at Lincoln on the approach to the Durham Ox crossing, with an afternoon train of empties. Guard's van next to the engine will be noted. *Photomatic*

116
'J11' No 5304 is at Frodingham Loco on 17 June 1934. The shed frontage, made of reinforced concrete, is of interest. *H. N. James*

12 Grimsby Fish

No description of the GC would be really complete without some mention of the fish traffic. The location of Grimsby, Britain's principal fishing port, at the north-east corner of the system ensured the company a place among the chief carriers of fish in the country. There was a certain amount of competition for the London traffic with the Great Northern Railway, whose access to Grimsby by means of the East Lincolnshire line offered a more direct route to the capital, but apart from this the GC held a dominant position, and at 1923 were despatching approximately eight complete fish trains daily from the docks, bound variously for London, Manchester, Liverpool, the Midlands and the West Country. This did not include fish vans attached to the rear of passenger trains; a considerable number left Grimsby every day in this manner, and some trains carried a greater tonnage of fish wagons than they did of passenger stock. However, under a rationalisation plan put into effect in 1924 the London traffic was transferred to the GN Section, running via the East Lincolnshire line and Peterborough as the GN fish trains had done in pre-Grouping days; as well as offering a quicker route to London, this arrangement also had the merit of avoiding the very congested section of GC line between Doncaster and Sheffield.

The fish trains were mostly fully braked and ran at passenger train speeds. Great punctuality of working was observed so as to ensure prompt delivery of the highly perishable cargo. To assist in this, trains were limited to a specific number of wagons, although at busy times these would sometimes be exceeded. By 1923 the engines used on the heavier fish trains were the powerful Class 9Q 4-6-0s, now known as Class B7, although the original 'Fish' engines, now Class B5, also took a share in some of the workings. From about 1928 the LNER-designed 'J39' engines, nicknamed 'Standards', were used a good deal, and in the late 1930s 'K3' 2-6-0s. The sheds mainly involved with the work were Gorton, Immingham and Woodford.

In this chapter two specific trains are described, both being in many respects typical of the traffic as a whole.

The 6.27pm departure from Grimsby Docks carried consignments of fish for the West Country. These arrived at their ultimate destinations via the GWR after being handed over at Banbury, and to reach the latter the train took an interesting route. Travelling via Lincoln, it traversed the comparatively little-known Barnetby-Lincoln section of the GC, passing through such remote and countrified stations as Moortown, Snelland and Langworth. At Lincoln it joined the LD&EC line, reaching the GC main line at Kirkby South Junction, and proceeded thence to Banbury in the usual way. Stops for examination, putting off and attaching of vehicles were made at Pyewipe West (Lincoln), Nottingham Victoria, and Leicester Central; a stop for water was made at Mansfield station. The tendency for this train, as for other fish trains, to call at passenger stations is an indication of

the fact that for operating purposes they were largely regarded as passenger trains, but those individuals who happened to be on the platforms at the times when such arrivals took place would not have been likely to think much of the idea, as the smell which accompanied the fish trains was usually fairly pungent! Arrival at Banbury was at 12.5am, and here the train was broken up by the GWR, one portion being taken southward along the Reading line and the other going in the direction of Swindon.

Between Grimsby and Banbury the train was worked by the LNER, one engine covering the whole distance without change. Both crew and locomotive hailed from Woodford; they were on their way home after lodging at Grimsby, having made the outward trip in the very early hours of the morning with a Woodford-Grimsby mixed train of goods and empties. The size of the fish train varied, this being subject of course to the volume of fish landed on any given day. The working timetables of 1924 stipulate a maximum load of 30 vans, but as already mentioned these official limits were sometimes exceeded; thus for instance vans of pigs were sometimes attached at Pyewipe West for conveyance to Messrs Harris's sausage factory at Calne in Wiltshire. The 1927 timetable however gives a limit of 37 vans, the increase possibly being due to the use of more powerful engines.

Having come off the train at Banbury, the Woodford men had completed their evening's work and were timetabled to return light to their home shed, but occasionally there were a few wagons waiting at Banbury to be taken at the earliest opportunity to the north and these would be brought to Woodford for attaching to a northbound goods. Quite often these vehicles contained biscuits from the Reading factories of Messrs Huntley & Palmers and Peek Frean. Official arrival at Woodford was 2.10am. In the 1930s the return working from Banbury became a regular part of the diagram, with an arrival back at Woodford at 2.7am; this return train was picked up at Banbury Junction at 1.40am after the engine had run back light from the passenger station. This increased activity probably reflects the growth of traffic on the Woodford-Banbury link, which was very much a feature of the GC scene during this period.

To work both ends of the turn on a day-to-day basis Woodford had of course to supply two engines and sets of men; such jobs were usually referred to as 'double-enders'. The working began late on Sunday evening when the first crew booked on to work the down empties and goods to Grimsby; this left Woodford at 1.20am and was due at Grimsby at 8.5 the next morning. The men then lodged during the day, booking on again about 5pm to work home with the fish. The second set of men would come on duty on Monday evening to work to Grimsby and so it would go on through the week, with each crew completing three out-and-back trips.

At the Grimsby end of the line arrangements were

made for the engine to be taken to Immingham for stabling as the facilities at the small local shed were not adequate for this purpose. The Woodford crew were therefore relieved by Immingham men and the engine made the lengthy run to Immingham shed, going back along the main line as far as Grimsby West Marsh and then branching off to traverse three or four miles of the Grimsby Light Railway; the Woodford men were usually relieved at Grimsby Docks. In the evening the reverse procedure took place. An Immingham crew booked on at 4.27pm to prepare the fish engine, taking it out at 5.27, and handing over to the main line men at Grimsby Docks or Grimsby Town station. The job of preparing the engine and taking it to the docks was known at Immingham as 'Banbury E&T'; the letters stood for 'engine and tender' and this expression was often used on the GC to denote jobs which involved preparation of locomotives.

The Woodford men thus had no additional burdens to worry about at the Grimsby end, and once they had been relieved by the local crew it was but a short step to their lodgings. There was no enginemen's barracks at Grimsby, and instead they found accommodation with one of the many railway families in the vicinity of Grimsby Loco. In most cases such an arrangement was preferable to sleeping at a barracks, and an added advantage was that they could visit the fish docks during the day, where freshly-caught fish could be brought for a trifling sum; it was a frequent practice to buy a 28lb bass of fish for five shillings, all of which could be resold at a good profit back home. The system of lodging at Grimsby was in all probability a relic of the days before Immingham was built.

Guards' workings operated in a similar way. The Woodford man who climbed aboard at the beginning of the trip came right through to Grimsby and lodged in the same way as the footplatemen, also going back on the fish. Two guards were of course needed to cover a week's working, and with guards as with enginemen the job was a popular one.

Between the wars the engines used on these turns were, so far as is known, invariably of GC origin. There is however evidence, particularly in the earlier years, of a rather curious utilisation of engines at Woodford during this period. Up to the mid-1920s at least, the locomotives regularly used on fish services were, somewhat surprisingly, Class C4 Atlantics. These were of course among the best GC-designed express passenger types, and in their prime never worked on any other kind of job apart from this curious interlude at Woodford. And to make the situation still more strange, a number of the shed's best passenger turns were worked at the same time by Class B7 4-6-0s, a type that at any other shed would have been regarded as highly suitable for fish work. The authority for this curious reversal of roles is obscure, and the decision could have emanated either from the shed management or the District Headquarters at Neasden. What is certain is that it was not popular with the men; the Atlantics were highly thought of at Woodford, as elsewhere, and the crews considered that they were wasted on fish trains.

Further evidence of the same policy became apparent

in 1926 following the arrival of the two Class B1 4-6-0 engines in April. Identical with the Atlantics in every respect apart from the rear pair of coupled wheels, and designed purely for passenger work, they were nevertheless put to regular use on the fish trains. Like the Atlantics they were considered to be excellent passenger engines, and their use on any less exalted work was deplored by the footplatemen; some of the drivers even preferred them to the Atlantics because, with the greater adhesion deriving from the extra pair of coupled wheels, they were capable of smart starting.

The men's views availed little in respect of either class however, and the only concession to such feelings was that as far as the Atlantics were concerned, it was usually the ones that were getting run-down and due for overhaul which were rostered for the fish turns, the others being kept for more suitable work. The situation improved a little from the mid-1920s with a modest influx of genuine mixed-traffic types in the shape of the Class B5 4-6-0s, but occasional use of the Atlantics on fish is known to have continued even into the 1930s and the advent of the 'B5s' appears to have made no difference whatever to the frequent rostering of 'B1s' for this work.

At Grouping Woodford's Atlantics were Nos 5194, 5260-3, 5362 and 6085/8/91/3/4, a mixture of superheated and saturated engines. Despite the presence of a number of 'B7s' they are believed to have monopolised the fish turns until the arrival of the two 'B1s', Nos 5195/6. As is remarked in Part 2B of Locomotives of the LNER, the latter seem to have had a rather nomadic existence up to this time, but from the day of their arrival at Woodford their wanderings were over and they were to settle down there until the war, putting in many appearances on the Grimsby fish turns. They reached Woodford in the spring of 1926.

It was during 1926 that Woodford also received its first 'B5s', Nos 5184/6. With a driving-wheel diameter of 6ft 1in, and belonging to the original 'Fish' class of pre-1914 days, they were in every way more suitable for fish work than either of the types previously used, and were soon put to work alongside the two 'B1s'. The four engines formed a somewhat curious quartet, with the black goods livery of the 'B5s' contrasting sharply against the sparkling passenger green of their stablemates, not to mention the noticeable difference in driving-wheel diameter.

Because there were other fish and goods turns to be covered besides the Grimsby work, there were barely enough 4-6-0s to cover the requirements, and if one of them failed or was out of traffic for some reason it would have been necessary to turn once again to the faithful if somewhat unsuitable Atlantics; however 'B7' engines were also used on occasion, as for example on Thursday 8 December 1927 when No 5038 took the empties to Grimsby with Driver Sam Smith at the regulator. The more powerful 'B7' may have been chosen in anticipation of a heavier load on the Friday, this being traditionally a day of heavy demand for fish.

The use of unsuitable substitutes would have declined considerably after July 1928, when two more 'B5s' were transferred to Woodford. These were Nos 6068/71, and the number of two-cylinder 4-6-0s then settled down at six for several years, the only change being the replacement of No 5184 by 5180 of the same class in July 1929.

Such records as have been traced show a remarkably consistent pattern or working. The earliest date which can be quoted is 15 January 1927, when 'B5' No 5186 arrived at Grimsby with the empties; this was at the very beginning of the switch-over from Atlantics, with the two original 'B5s' being comparative newcomers. Evidence of the partnership with the larger-wheeled 'B1s' is seen in the recollections of a former Woodford footplateman, who remembers making his first trip to Grimsby as a young fireman on 30 September 1927; his mate was Sam Smith and the engine 'B1' No 5195, resplendent in green passenger livery.

Notes of a full six days' working have been preserved for the week beginning Monday 18 February 1929, when 'B5' No 5184 went to Grimsby, followed by another of the class, No 6071, on the next day. These two then alternated on the turn during the rest of the week, showing that the usual system of working was for the two crews on the Grimsby job to keep to the same engines, at least for that week. This was after the arrival of the second pair of 'B5s' at Woodford, and they no doubt appeared regularly on the Grimsby turn, but it must not be supposed that they monopolised it, for on the six days beginning 15 July, five months later, 'B1' No 5196 worked opposite 'B5' No 6068, the latter going on the first day. No 6068 was on the job again a month later, being noted on 19 and 21 August, while on the four days from 17 to 20 December Nos 5186 and 6071 worked together, No 5186 taking the Monday turn.

Some indication of the very regular pattern of working can be seen in the fact that as late as 1935 the same engines were still being used. From July 1929 the allocation of Woodford 'B5s' remained completely unchanged for more than five years, and so we find that on Monday 30 September 1935 'B1' No 5195 worked to Grimsby, alternating through the rest of the week with 'B5' No 5180. Although no notes have come to light covering the intervening period, it is likely that between them these two types monopolised all the fish work performed at Woodford. Introduced as Class 8 as early as 1902, the 'B5s' had been specially designed for express fish work, and their continuing use on this work over 30 years later is an indication of the soundness of J. G. Robinson's original concept.

By the end of 1935 however their days on the Grimsby fish were numbered. The transfer of a batch of Class K3 2-6-0s to Gorton for fast goods work in the autumn of that year released a like number of the well-tried 'B7s', some of which were sent to Woodford. Arriving there between October 1935 and January 1937, they more than doubled the shed's allocation of that type. They quickly found their way on to the Grimsby turn, evidence of them having supplanted the two-cylinder engines being seen in the transfer of 'B5s' Nos 5186 and 6068 to Sheffield in March 1936. The remaining 'B5s' and the two 'B1s' are not likely to have found much employment on the fish

turns after this date. Diary records of the period immediately following indicate a regular pattern of 'B7' working, as the following examples show: 12 September 1936, 'B7' No 5481; 7 October, 'B7' No 5464; 7 November, 'B7' No 5464; 2 January 1937, 'B7' No 5078; 17 May, 'B7' No 5463. In all probability they had a monopoly of the job until they eventually left Woodford during the war. The last time that Woodford crews lodged at Grimsby before the practice was terminated because of war conditions was 9 November 1942, when Driver Hollis and Fireman Marriott worked the empties with 'B7' No 5484.

The campaign for improvements in engine utilisation which got under way in the mid-1930s has already been referred to in previous chapters, and the use of the 'B7s' at Woodford would permit the introduction of more flexible rostering, by which they could cover a considerable range of turns including the fish, thus eliminating the need to roster engines specially for the latter, which involved lengthy standing-time on Woodford shed. This would in all probability put an end to the long-standing pattern of working whereby the turn was shared by the same engines through the week.

The Woodford Fish Train Link was next in seniority to the Fast Passenger Link and in addition to the Grimsby jobs its members were responsible for a similar pair of fish turns to Doncaster, also involving lodging; a couple of out-and-home jobs were included in the link in the usual way, to give the men a rest from being continually away from home, although it is doubtful if these turns would be worked with the same engines as were used on the fish. It is possible that the link may not have been in existence in early LNER days, in which case the Grimsby job would have been worked on a regular basis by the same pair of drivers, perhaps because they were the only ones who knew the road at that time. Woodford drivers known to have worked on the Grimsby turn include Barrass, Raines, Smith, Hulls, E. Coulson, H. Coulson, Goodhand, and Bayes.

With about 60 goods guards allocated to Woodford during the period under review, there were no doubt many different occupants of the Grimsby fish brake-vans as time went on, but two men who are well remembered as having worked regularly on the job in early LNER days were Tom Collier and Jack Shillito; both apparently enjoyed the Grimsby job, and were in the habit of bringing back fish for sale at home.

The monopoly which was enjoyed on the Grimsby-Banbury trains by GC engines, crews and guards offers a good example of the way in which certain services, particularly those of a less well-known character, retained a completely unadulterated Great Central flavour in the interwar period, and the same is true of the Grimsby-Manchester trains which are described in the next section. Having been a Gorton responsibility for many years, the working of the 5.10pm fish from Grimsby Docks to Ashton Moss was altered in the mid-1930s to become an Immingham turn. Known as the 'First Fish' in Manchester because of the fact that it was followed by a later train from Grimsby, it had in earlier years been routed into Manchester Ducie Street, but was switched to Ashton Moss about 1929; the regular appearance of Gorton engines on it for so many years made the change-over to those of a different shed seem like the end of an era.

Neither the reason for this change nor the date of it can be given with any certainty, although it appears that there had been some complaints by Gorton men about the inconvenience of lodging at Immingham Loco. Anyone familiar with Immingham in the days before 1939 will understand this attitude, as it was an extremely isolated spot, and the hours of enforced idleness spent there during lodging would undoubtedly grate on the Gorton men, accustomed to the familiar bustle of Ashton Old Road. For their part, the Immingham men still had a vivid memory of how, as a result of the reorganisation mentioned at the beginning of this chapter they had been forced to yield up their crack workings, the London fish trains, to the GN men from New England. That was in 1924, and since then they had been reduced to a humble relieving role as far as fish was concerned, such as has been described in connection with the Banbury fish; they were therefore keen to restore something of their original dominance if at all possible, and when after discussion it was found that no satisfactory scheme of sharing the work between Gorton and Immingham could be agreed on, they were more than willing to step into the breach and take over the complete set of workings. They thus benefited substantially by this arrangement, acquiring a 'double-ender' lodging turn to Manchester and associated weekend working into the bargain.

Probably the best clue to the date is to be found in the details of engine transfers. On 1 January 1936, 'B7' No 5476 was switched from Gorton to Immingham, followed four days later by a sister engine, No 5477. With 'B7s' Nos 5467/78 already there, Immingham now had ample power to cover the Manchester workings. The 'B7s' were the most suitable GC type for heavy fish work, having long been used by Gorton on these very turns that had now been acquired by their colleagues in Lincoln-shire, and the transfer of Nos 5476/77 was clearly a move of some importance, especially as these were of the later short-chimney type. For want of more precise informa-tion, therefore, it appears that the Manchester working began in the early weeks of 1936, and the earliest exact date so far traced is Monday, 10 February, when Driver Alf Wilson and Fireman David Baker worked to Manchester with 'B7' No 5476, one of the original Immingham pair.

Despite many dubious notices in the popular railway press over the years, the 'B7s' were greatly liked by the GC men. The derogatory nickname 'Black Pig' which is said to have been applied to them and which is almost monotonously repeated in railway publications, was entirely unknown among the GC staff, to whom they were always 'Four-cylinders'. Whatever the men's experience of the type might have been, loyalty alone would have forbade the use of such an opprobrious term, in view of the men's well-known partiality for Gorton products. Judged by the somewhat narrow standards of

certain technical writings, the coal consumption of the 'B7s' was undoubtedly high, but it is not likely that ques-tions of fuel economy were much in consideration at the time they were designed, while the task of firing them was well within the compass of a generation of men selected with an eye to physical suitability and, in the words of Mr S. C. Townroe, 'trained to keep the pressure on the mark.' The four 'B7s' based at Immingham in the late 1930s appear to have given every satisfaction, just as Gorton's large allocation of the class had done in earlier years.

As for appearance, the 'B7s' have received little acclaim in published accounts, where the praises of the 'Jersey Lily' Atlantics are usually sung; yet it has become evident that the 'B7s' were much admired by observers. The authors have been surprised at the number of people who, when asked to delve into their recollections con-cerning the appearance of Robinson engines, have singled out the 'B7' as a machine of exceptionally attractive lines. It is possible that the published preference for the 'Jersey Lilies' reflects a southerly bias, for these engines were a very common sight on the high-speed trains south of Leicester, whereas the small number of 'B7s' based in that part of the world, or visiting it, were usually employed on night-time duties, or at best on very humdrum turns which hardly showed them off to advantage.

The commencement of Immingham working on the 5.10pm ex-Grimsby was in one sense a means whereby the 'B7s' were able to remain in the limelight to some extent, for at Gorton they were fast being displaced on the best turns by 'K3' 2-6-0s. The switch of responsibility therefore allowed them to retain a hold on at least one of the recognised top-flight workings.

The Immingham working began on the Monday after-noon, when the first of the two crews rostered to go to Manchester signed on at the Loco at 2.54pm, and having prepared their engine for departure exactly one hour later they set off tender-first for New Clee sidings, where the fish trains were marshalled. By 4.45 they had taken hold of a substantial train of fish vans, often loaded to the maximum of 45 vehicles and were waiting for the right-away. Because of the scheduled call at Doncaster Mars-hgate for remarshalling, the 5.10 was routed via the South Yorkshire line instead of going via Retford and Sheffield as did the through passenger trains to Manchester; this more direct route took the train through Wath and Wombwell, along the Worsborough branch to avoid Barnsley, and finally on to the GC main line at Barnsley Junction. After calling at Marshgate, where it was examined and there was interchange with fish from Hull, the train made only stops for water until reaching Godley, where vehicles for the CLC were detached. One of the water stops was at Wentworth, where banking assistance was provided either by the Garratt or by the engines working in its place. Further vehicles were taken off at Guide Bridge, and the remainder of the train then reached Ashton Moss by means of the right-hand junction immediately beyond Guide Bridge station; here it was finally handed over to the LMS. The usual standard of punctuality was scrupulously maintained, and staff on the Woodhead line have often made the same remark about the 'First Fish' — 'you could set your watch by it'. The total time allowed for the journey was 6hr 20min, the difficulty of the work varying according to the load, which of course reflected the differences in daily landings of fish at Grimsby.

Normally the Immingham men were relieved at Guide Bridge as their road knowledge did not cover the Ashton Moss line, and consequently the previous situation whereby Immingham men had played second fiddle to the incoming Gorton crews at Grimsby was exactly reversed at this end, with the Manchester men performing the mundane task of providing relief. Sometimes however no crew was available for this, and in that case the trainmen had to continue to Ashton Moss with a local pilotman on board.

Coming off at Guide Bridge in the usual way, the Immingham men walked to Gorton Loco or hitched a lift on a passing train; their ultimate destination of course was the barracks on Cornwall Street. It was usually midnight or later when they reached it, and one imagines that a fireman who had forgotten what it was like to spend a shift on a 'B7', or was new to the class, would be glad to get his head on the pillow.

Unless the Immingham men had gone through to Ashton Moss, the engine would be brought in by the relief crew, who then carried out the usual loco duties, or handed it over to a shed crew for this purpose. Once this task had been finished the engine was then berthed in its appointed place and remained untouched until required the following afternoon; engines working on the fish trains were normally kept strictly to their diagrams unless a failure occurred, and so the Immingham men almost invariably went back with their own machine.

For the return trip the men booked on at 2.20 in the afternoon. With the engine already prepared, they had only to climb on board after the usual 15min for notices, whistle for the road, and trundle the few hundred yards down to Ashburys Yard, there to couple up to the three o'clock Ashburys-Grimsby Class A Goods. This was a considerably more leisurely working than the fish, as its 'A' classification implies, and the train made a variety of stops en route before eventually reaching Grimsby towards 1am. It got off to a very slow start, with calls at Dewsnap Yard and Godley consuming over an hour altogether; at both places the original modest load was added to, the Godley vehicles having come off the CLC. On the other side of the Pennines the better-known but longer route via Retford was taken, with lengthy stops at Worksop and Retford Whisker Hill; at the former, train examination held up progress for more than an hour.

On the last stretch to Grimsby the crew were often relieved by men travelling out specially from Immmingham, so that excessive overtime would not be accumulated; such relief usually took place at Barnetby, and from there the trainmen would continue the journey in the brake-van. Many of the Immingham men lived in Grimsby, but those unfortunates whose homes were near Immingham Loco faced another journey of several miles when the train finally wound its way into the sidings at Grimsby Docks.

The 3.00 Ashburys-Grimsby is one of those trains which, had the development of Grimsby and Immingham gone the way the original company wished, would have attained greater importance than it did. So far as the western side of the Pennines is concerned, it is best remembered as providing the unforgettable spectacle of a 'B7' climbing uninterruptedly to Woodhead, something that by 1936 was a great deal less common than it had been.

Shortly after the homegoing crew had boarded their engine in Gorton Loco Yard, a second Immingham crew were coming on duty to perform the Tuesday/Wednesday working, and so the process went on through the week. However at weekends the pattern altered, and the turns worked on Saturday and Sunday are of considerable interest.

The original Grimsby crew of Monday reappeared at Gorton on Friday night, but as the Ashburys-Grimsby did not run on Saturdays they were diagrammed for a rather different return trip. They worked the Sunday 1.30am newspaper and mails express from Manchester London Road, this along with its weekday counterpart being known as the 'Morning Star'. As they were not due to come on duty until 11.55pm the Immingham men had to spend all Saturday at Gorton; the reason for the rather curious booking-on time was that by starting the job before midnight the company were able to class it as a Saturday working, and so avoid paying Sunday overtime rates.

The 1.30am consisted almost entirely of parcels vehicles crammed with Sunday papers from the Manchester presses, together with mail and sundry parcels; for belated travellers, one or two coaches were provided, usually marshalled behind the tender. There was a lengthy halt at Sheffield during which the train was completely remarshalled; vans of papers and mail were attached here for numerous stations on the Cleethorpes road, for the express from Manchester now became, in effect, a stopping train, calling almost everywhere east of Sheffield. On this section two guards were carried, to share the task of throwing out bundles at each stop.

A curiosity of the working was that as the train neared Grimsby a fresh engine was taken out of Immingham Loco to meet it and the respective crews switched over, the trainmen remaining in charge, but on a different engine. The purpose of this was to release the valuable 'B7' for other work during the morning, and depending on what was envisaged the change-over could take place at Brocklesby, Barnetby, or even as far afield as Retford. On Sunday 16 February 1936, at the end of the first recorded week of Immingham working, Driver Wilson and Fireman Baker worked the turn with 'B7' No 5477.

The men who came into Manchester with the Saturday evening fish were more fortunate than their opposite numbers in having a much shorter stop-over. They were on duty again at 3.29 on the Sunday afternoon, and after reading notices were allowed a few minutes' walking-time to Gorton & Openshaw station where they waited for the 3.35 Manchester London Road-Sheffield passenger train. Taking over from the local relief crew who were on the footplate, they set off on the first stage of the long haul home. On this initial stretch they were working tender-first, as the train was booked to call at Glossop, where the engine would change ends. The process of running round the train in the little terminus was a major intrusion into the peace and tranquility of a spot which was quiet enough at any time, and considerably more so at four o' clock on a Sunday afternoon. In those days the station was overlooked by a large Wesleyan Reform Church on Howard Street, and no doubt the arrival of this unaccustomedly large and noisy visitor was regarded by the worthy churchgoers as little less than a profanation of the Sabbath, especially as its visit coincided with the time of the weekly Sunday school service.

After reaching Sheffield the engine and train remained for more than an hour before recommencing the journey, this time as the 7pm Sheffield-Cleethorpes, calling at very nearly all stations en route to achieve an eventual arrival in Cleethorpes at 10.13. Having taken the engine to Immingham Loco and disposed it the men were usually able to get away shortly before midnight.

The final turn to be chronicled in the complete pattern of workings is the Sunday outward trip which brought an Immingham engine and crew into Manchester to return next day with the Ashburys-Grimsby goods. For this the men booked on at 2.30pm on Sunday, prepared their engine and worked the 4.40 Cleethorpes-Manchester passenger as far as Sheffield, where engines were changed; this was booked to call nearly everywhere and was timed to reach Sheffield at 7.25, a Gorton engine and men taking over for the final leg into Manchester. The Immingham men followed at 7.50 with another typical Sunday evening passenger train, calling at most stations on the Woodhead line including Glossop, which thus received its second 'B7' visitation of the day. Arrival at Manchester London Road was at 9.58, and after retiring to Gorton Loco the crew settled down to yet another of the long stop-overs which were a feature of these turns, not being needed until the middle of the next afternoon.

The amount of time spent lodging betrays the fact that turns were originally worked from the Gorton end, as under the original arrangements the Manchester men would have been at home during these long spells off duty. Such inconvenience was a price the Immingham men were more than willing to pay for possession of these lucrative jobs and, as was ever the case with lodging turns, the long hours away from home suited some more than others. To be obliged to spend the whole of Saturday kicking one's heels in a strange place hardly sounds an entertaining prospect, but for a man brought up in a small village such as Immingham was in those days, Manchester could offer many interesting diversions. In the field of sport, which probably exerted a stronger hold over working people than it has done in more recent times, there was in the appropriate seasons First Division soccer, county and sometimes Test cricket, racing, dogs, wrestling, and speedway, the last three only 10min walk away at Belle Vue. For those not attracted to sport, the shops and cinemas of the city centre could be sampled for

the sake of hitching a ride to London Road. One of the Immingham drivers is remembered as having been exceptionally fond of tripe, that celebrated Lancashire delicacy, and was in the habit of boarding his engine with a parcel under his arm, the contents of which had usually been consumed before the train reached Sheffield.

The links were organised so that one of the two sets of men actually began their roster on the Sunday afternoon, working to Manchester with the 4.40pm passenger and then going through the week opposite the crew who had started on Monday with the fish. The odd Saturday/Sunday turn — out with fish, home with the 3.35pm passenger — was usually performed by a third crew who had made two lodging trips to Sheffield earlier in the week with the 'Butter Train', a heavy braked goods similar to the fish. Immingham drivers known to have performed the Manchester workings include Tommy Joyce, George Bishop, Alf Wilson, Tom Steadman, Harry Goodhand, T. White and J. Welton. The work took them further afield than any of their colleagues except those working to Kings Cross on the Easons' turns, and they were well in line for promotion to the express passenger link when vacancies came up.

Guards' workings on the fish and goods turns corresponded closely to the enginemen's and they lodged at Gorton in the same way. In the years before the outbreak of war it is probable that they would have the opportunity of riding in the latest 'Queen Marys', the long-wheelbase brake vans specially developed by the LNER for fast goods work and said to give a very comfortable ride. Despite this it is doubtful if the Manchester job was a particularly popular one, at least during the winter; keeping warm was a constant fight in the draughty vans, especially on fast trains, and as the fish was timed to pass Dunford in nice time for the evening frost to have set in it is likely that the unfortunate guard was chilled to the bone by the time Guide Bridge was reached.

As a final glimpse at the fish train, we note a few occasions when probably on account of reduced loads it was not worked by the customary 'B7'. After Christmas 1936 two 'J39' 0-6-0s were noted, No 1273 on 28 December and 1967 two days later, the loads probably being smaller than usual because of the holiday period. 'B5' No 5187 turned up on 22 May 1937, going back on the Sunday turn the next day, but appearances of this type were rare. A little over a week later, on Wednesday 2 June, 'J39' No 1492 came into Manchester with Driver J. Welton at the regulator.

Like the Banbury workings described earlier, the Grimsby-Manchester jobs are of historical interest in being among the last top-flight turns regularly worked by the 'B7' 4-6-0s, which were now coming to the end of their career on GC fast goods trains. Immingham were still using them for the Manchester job at the outbreak of war, although by this time No 5476 had gone back to Gorton and been replaced by No 5034; before very long the whole class was to be gathered at Gorton and down-graded to various humdrum duties, which meant that their days as main line engines were over.

117
'B1' No 5195, often used on the Woodford fish trains, is at its home shed about 1931. *G. Coltas*

118
Another view of No 5195 at Woodford about the same time. *G. Coltas*

119
'B5' No 6068 at Woodford Loco about 1931. These engines did the bulk of Woodford's fish work until the mid-1930s. *G. Coltas*

120
Another class much used on fish work at the northern end of the GC system were the 'J39s'. No 2966 is seen on Leicester Loco about 1930. *G. Coltas*

119

120

121

122

121
The versatile 'four-cylinders' were as much at home on express passenger trains as on fish. Here is No 5484 on an up fast at Staverton Road in the late 1930s. *G. Coltas*

122
This view of No 5180 at Woodford shed shows the handsome lines of the early Robinson 4-6-0s. *G. Coltas*

123

123
The unlikely use of Atlantics on fish work continued into the 1930s. No 6093 approaches Bagthorpe junction on an up train on 2 June 1932.
T. G. Hepburn/Rail Archive Stephenson

124
The 'N5s' were a good deal less common at the southern end of the GC. No 5987 shunts at Woodford Loco about 1931. *G. Coltas*

125
'B5' No 6071 of Woodford waits at Banbury with a
northbound special on a summer Sunday evening in 1936.
C. R. L. Coles

126
Transferred to Immingham in 1936, 'B7' No 5476 is seen at
Gorton Loco in earlier times. *Real Photographs*

125

126

127
'B5' No 5186 is at Woodford with the C&W Dept shops in the background. A view taken about 1931. *G. Coltas*

128
The same engine is in action at Nottingham Victoria on an up fish, about 1927. It is leaving the up loop after examination of the train.
T. G. Hepburn/Rail Archive Stephenson

129
The 'K2' engines were also much used on GC fish trains. No 4632 of Mexborough is seen at Woodford Loco.
G. Coltas

130
'J39' No 1273 worked on the Grimsby-Ashton Moss fish trains in the mid-1930s.   *Photomatic*

131
A pair of Woodford engines on an up fish at Bagthorpe Junction on 5 July 1932. 'B5' No 6068 pilots 'C4' No 5262.
T. G. Hepburn/Rail Archive Stephenson

131

13 The Annesley 'Dido'

Annesley's main claim to fame is that it was the spot, a few miles north of Nottingham, where the original MSLR system met the new London Extension, completed just before the turn of the century. Here, in the midst of green fields, and with few habitations in sight apart from the small mining village of Newstead, the GCR chose to build a locomotive shed. It is the belief of local railwaymen that the company's original choice of site was Bulwell, in the northern suburbs of Nottingham, but because of the rather high rates demanded by the Corporation for development in this area, new plans were drawn up for a more distant location at Annesley, which as well as being cheaper had the advantage of offering plenty of room for further expansion — an important consideration in view of the expectations which were entertained for the newly built line to London.

An additional bonus was that the shed was conveniently adjacent to Annesley marshalling yard, where traffic from surrounding collieries was assembled for conveyance both to north and south. The shed's main purpose was to supply the heavy mineral engines for these trains, and also smaller engines to operate the numerous trips to and from the collieries. Within a fairly short time of opening, Annesley also became responsible for providing passenger engines for a number of main line trains when the original 'passenger' shed at Arkwright Street, on the southern side of Nottingham, was found to be too costly to maintain and was closed.

These considerable advantages were purchased at a certain cost. In an age when railwaymen, in common with most workers, usually resided within easy walking-distance of their place of employment, the out-of-the-way location of Annesley Loco was a definite drawback. The nearest residential areas were Bulwell, Hucknall, and Kirkby, all of them several miles away, and it was clear from the beginning that unless the company were prepared to build their own settlement, as they had done for example at Woodford, the only alternative would be to provide a frequent and convenient means of travel to and from the new establishment. Hence the Annesley 'Dido', which had begun life as a train conveying workmen and materials at the time the site was under development.

Perhaps in the early days the company hoped that the presence of the Loco and yards would, in the fullness of time, create its own residential development in the vicinity, so that the need for a staff train would eventually disappear, but if such expectations were ever entertained they were not to be fulfilled. Throughout GCR and LNER days Annesley was to remain the same isolated backwater, pleasant enough in its setting of open fields on a warm summer day, somewhat bleak and inhospitable in the winter. Its shortcomings were probably more apparent to those unfortunate employees who were called on to lodge at the place; following its usual practice the company provided a barracks for visiting crews, this being in the shape of a large single-storey wooden

structure, faintly resembling a string of cricket pavilions, which at a fairly early stage seems to have acquired a distinctly dilapidated appearance. Running water was non-existent, and all drinking-water requirements had to be supplied by the transport of Nottingham Corporation water from Bulwell; this process added a picturesque touch, insofar as for many years the water was conveyed in old Sacre locomotive tenders. The comfort of resting enginemen was further prejudiced by the fact that, despite the considerable spaces about the premises, the planners had seen fit to locate the barracks directly alongside the shed roads, which of course meant that peace and quiet could be sampled only at short intervals between the whistling and clanking of locomotives, the rattle of couplings, and all the other assorted noises associated with a busy running shed. All these discomforts, coupled with the complete absence of any form of social facilities in the surrounding district, gave Annesley Loco a villainous reputation among GC enginemen. So untouched by any form of modern development did the place remain, indeed, that even after World War 2 the only improvement was that the drinking-water was transported in glass-lined tanks, instead of old tenders. Introduced perhaps as a temporary expedient, the 'Dido' had come to stay.

The importance of the 'Dido' may best be judged by the number of people employed at Annesley Loco and the nearby yard. By Grouping about 70 engines were allocated to Annesley shed, and the total workforce, covering a variety of grades which included footplatemen, cleaners, tradesmen, and shed labourers as well as the supervisory and administrative staffs was in the region of 500. The number of goods guards and yard staff based at Annesley Yard was probably in excess of 100, while Bulwell-based guards also had to travel on the 'Dido' when working turns that finished at Annesley. There was also a Carriage and Wagon shop employing a substantial team of men. Taking all this into account, it is probable that the number of railwaymen regularly using the 'Dido' on a weekly basis was not far short of 1,000.

At Grouping the main residential area for GC staff was Bulwell, and by this time the place had also acquired some importance in the operating sphere, as it had become a point of interchange with the neighbouring GNR system. Traffic development had necessitated the provision of a marshalling yard, and the place had become a signing-on point for GC enginemen, many crews starting and finishing their turns of duty at Bulwell Common station. These developments were perhaps somewhat ironic in view of the decision to abandon the original plan of building the engine shed at Bulwell. The concentration of GCR employees in the neighbourhood meant that, after originally plying between Annesley and Kirkby, in the Mansfield direction, the 'Dido' was switched to work south of the former, terminating at Bulwell Common. By the summer of 1924 there were 19

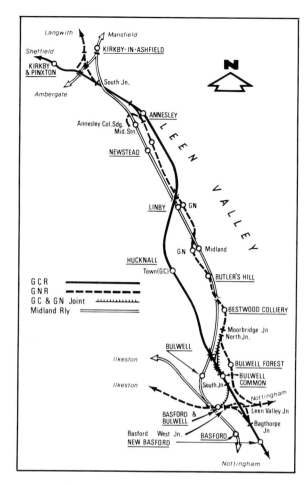

Fig 3
Map of the Annesley and Bulwell districts as in 1913. This was essentially unaltered by the Grouping. Annesley locomotive shed and yard were situated between the GC and GN lines south of Annesley Junction

survived long enough to put in a few turns of duty under LNER ownership. Its place may well have been taken by No 449B, one of the diminutive Sacre 2-4-0 tanks, which was noted on the 'Dido' at about this time; this engine had been employed on motor-train duty in the Neasden district, as briefly related in Chapter 8, but probably finished its time on the 'Dido', as it was withdrawn in the autumn of 1924. The next generation of Sacre veterans to operate the 'Dido' were the 4-4-0s, classed 'D12' by the LNER; several were in residence at Annesley by Grouping, and over the next few years they were to be in regular charge of the Dido, the ones noted being Nos 438B, 442B, 443B, 444B and 6466. These eminent Victorians, veterans of many a tough trip over Woodhead in the 1880s and 1890s, were highly typical of that era with their outside frames and rudimentary cabs, and strongly resembled the Midland Railway Kirtley engines of similar vintage. Such splendid relics of the MSLR heyday attracted considerable attention from observers, and it is likely that in a more railway-conscious era one of the class would have been preserved; had that come to pass, the choice would probably have fallen on No 6464, formerly 442B, which lasted until the early months of 1930, still on the 'Dido', and gained the distinction of being the last Sacre-designed passenger engine to be taken out of service.

As usual, the footplatemen had somewhat less romantic views about the old engines, and were not happy about the rather exposed cabs, which in a somewhat open location such as Annesley Loco would no doubt have been decidedly draughty. Weatherboards had been fitted to the tenders by 1923, but even with this refinement the 'D12s' were still distinctly spartan machines; no doubt the chief value of the weatherboards was felt during the frequent tender-first trips, which were a necessity because there was not enough time to use the Annesley turntable while waiting there. The engine usually faced north, running tender-first towards Bulwell.

The 'Dido' was worked in three shifts, the crews signing on at Annesley at 6.25am, 2.25pm and 10.25pm. A number of the drivers were men in the final years of their service who had applied to work the 'Dido' as a means of comfortably finishing their time away from the rigours of main line work. These venerable individuals, paired with young firemen rising through the normal promotional sequence, would have put in a span of service closely comparable with that of the Sacre engines they drove, and when in talkative mood were no doubt capable of regaling their youthful mates with tales which one would give a lot to hear today.

As for the stock, few railway companies believed in providing unnecessarily high standards of comfort for their employees, regardless of grade, and neither the GCR nor the LNER were any exception. The two six-wheel coaches which comprised the normal 'Dido' set, if it could

trains making the five-mile journey between Bulwell Common and Annesley each weekday, with a corresponding number in the opposite direction. On the outward trip the trains terminated at Annesley sidings, which was between the Loco and the Carriage and Wagon shop. Based of course at Annesley Loco, the engine and stock was employed right round the clock, leaving Annesley at 12.15am daily for its first trip to Bulwell, and making its final return journey to Annesley sidings at 11.35pm, arriving 10 minutes later. The only break was on Sundays, when from the 7.45am arrival at Annesley until 11.50pm the train ran as required. Coaling and other duties were fitted in between trips, the train having three spells of over an hour at Annesley for this purpose.

During GCR days and for some time after, the 'Dido' duty was usually reserved for engines which, downgraded from more important duties, were eking out their last days of useful service. Before and during World War 1 there had been a number of Sacre 2-4-0s at Annesley, and these seem to have had quite a monopoly of the 'Dido', although Parker 0-6-2 tanks were occasionally noted. By late GCR days the 2-4-0s had gone to their rest except for No 169B, which was not withdrawn until the middle of 1923 and may just have be dignified by such a term, were a long way past their prime, although admittedly perhaps a little better than the oil-lit four-wheelers, with wooden seats, which were used on miners' trains in Chesterfield and elsewhere. For the benefit of the Carriage and Wagon Works staff, the 7.35am departure from Bulwell Common was a five-coach formation, which returned from Annesley sidings at 5.10pm on weekdays, and about 1pm on Saturdays.

As to the curious nickname by which the service was widely known throughout its long career, there has been no shortage of suggested explanations. These include references to the legendary Queen Dido, involving somewhat doubtful comparisons between Annesley Loco and the ancient city of Carthage which she ruled; links with the poet Byron, whose family seat of Newstead Abbey was hardly a stone's throw from the shed; and supposed corruptions of the name Diadem Hill, this appellation belonging to an eminence overlooking the loco. The study of railway nicknames is bedevilled by all kinds of traps and pitfalls, and the authors cannot claim to be experts in it, but in general it has been found that such nicknames are allied to the events which happened to catch the public fancy at a particular time. By far the most important event which was contemporary with the commencement of the 'Dido' service was the Diamond Jubilee of Queen Victoria, and the most likely explanation seems to be that the name 'Dido' was in some way linked with Queen Victoria, possibly because of comparisons between her and the ancient Queen of Carthage. Traces of the nickname appear in the 1860s, and at the time of Queen Victoria's Golden Jubilee in 1877. In 1896 a Royal Navy cruiser under construction on the Clyde was to be named HMS *Dido* at its launching the following year, almost certainly in honour of the Queen, but made the headlines when the timber supports under the hull collapsed and caused the vessel to enter the water somewhat prematurely.

The 1924 service already described was considerably more intensive than that which had operated in early GCR days and even during the war, the main reason for its expansion being the introduction of the railwaymen's eight-hour day in 1919. With increases in traffic generally, it was becoming progressively more difficult to find paths for the now very frequent 'Dido' service, and the LNER began to consider making use of an alternative route. The former GNR line which made physical contact with the GC at Bulwell ran roughly parallel with the latter out to Newstead, a station immediately adjacent to Annesley Loco; it was thus equally convenient for the conveyance of GC staff from Bullwell, and had the advantage of being far less busy than the GC main line. By the summer of 1925, therefore, the 'Dido' had been switched to run mainly over the GN Section line; the only drawback to this arrangement was that, as a result of a rationalisation plan put into effect by the LNER very shortly after Grouping, the line was closed on Sundays, and so throughout that day the 'Dido' operated on its original route. This also applied to the workings of early Monday morning, as the GN Section signalboxes did not open until 6am. During weekdays certain trips continued to be made over the GC route to and from Annesley sidings, and with the stop-over time at the latter being longer than at Newstead it is presumed that these trips were inserted to enable locomotive duties to be carried out at Annesley shed, which was not of course directly accessible from Newstead.

A further development of 1925 was the introduction of an intermediate stop at Hucknall. This modest town had the advantage of being served by stations on both the GC and GN lines, not to mention a third on the Midland Railway, and so the 'Dido' was booked to call either at the former GC establishment, Hucknall Central, or at Hucknall Town; in common with a number of GC stations, Hucknall Central belied its name in being a considerable distance from the town, and was by far the least convenient of the three stations serving Hucknall. The calls at Hucknall were originally timetabled on an 'as required' basis, but in later years were shown as regular stops.

The comparatively limited traffic of the GN Section route may be deduced from the fact that in September 1931 the stations at Newstead and Hucknall Town were closed to passengers. Since Grouping the retention of facilities on the parallel lines north of Nottingham had clearly been a wasteful duplication, and the fact that the obvious rationalisation manoeuvre was delayed until as late as 1931 can only be ascribed to what has sometimes been called 'pre-Grouping mentality'. The closure of Hucknall Town and Newstead did not of course affect the staff, who continued to use them as before, thus in effect having their own private stations.

The changes of 1925 may be seen clearly in the operating details applicable in 1928. Of a total of 18 trips each way on weekdays, 14 were via the GN route and four by the GC; the whole of the Sunday service was worked on the GC line, and also the Monday morning trips up to 6am. The period from late Sunday evening into the early hours of Monday was a very busy time at Annesley because of the large number of mineral and goods trains which were booked to start during these hours, a situation which applied at all important sheds; between midnight and 6am the 'Dido' made six return trips, conveying footplatemen and staff on the early shift. These 1928 details highlight another small curiosity, namely that from 6am on Sundays the 'Dido' was not allowed to wait at Bulwell Common as it did during the week; closure of the two Bulwell Common signalboxes at six o'clock on Sunday morning meant that the points were set for through traffic, preventing the 'Dido' from clearing the main line, or the engine from running round. Having deposited its passengers at Bulwell, the train therefore continued forward another three-quarters of a mile or so to New Basford, where it was able to wait without obstructing the main line.

With the inevitable variations in times and in the number of trips, the 'Dido' service remained basically as described above throughout the years up to September 1939, even the Sunday operations involving New Basford continuing in force. The particular interest of the 'Dido' in this later period is to be found in the locomotive sphere, and here there were developments of a quite remarkable character, not to mention events unique on the GC Section.

The LNER interest in steam railcars seems to have been aroused soon after Grouping, and as a result of experience in 1925-7 with two early cars built by the Sentinel Co a batch of improved Sentinels was built in 1927-8, together with others of a somewhat different design produced by the Clayton Wagon Co of Lincoln; cars incorporating further improvements followed soon after. Probably the greatest attraction of the steam railcar was its cheapness in operation, and as increasing numbers of the cars came into service during 1928 the LNER naturally began to take note of various services on which they could profitably be used. A study of the 'Dido' indicated that savings of up to £20,000 could be achieved annually, mainly on account of the railcars' much lower coal and water consumption, and the fact that they could operate without a guard; furthermore they were easier to handle at stations, because changes in direction could be accomplished without shunting movements necessary for an engine to run round its train.

Unfortunately it has not been possible to discover exactly when the first LNER railcar was sent to Annesley, nor has its identity been satisfactorily established. Official records show that the first arrival was No 2122 *Railway*, one of the Clayton series, but according to a number of local witnesses this machine was preceded by another Clayton car, No 2130 *Bang Up*. The initial choice of this car seems a distinct possibility in view of its seating capacity, which was only 44, against 64 for the rest of the class; hence the management may have preferred to use it on a non-revenue-earning service. Its replacement by *Railway* in July 1929, if indeed it was at Annesley at this time, is perhaps an indication that the seating capacity was insufficient.

Railway, having possibly been chosen because of its name, remained at Annesley until May 1930. During this period the last of the Sacre 4-4-0s was withdrawn, and so the car would have had every opportunity of proving itself on the 'Dido', though it is probable that by this time it had come to be regarded as a failure. Both the Claytons were generally considered too weak for the work they had to do, and the banks on the GN route are said to have tested them severely; the railwaymen's verdict on *Bang Up* was that it was 'a poor thing', and *Railway* 'not much better'. A particularly serious drawback was that if the injectors failed the fire had to be immediately thrown out, and the machine was thus immobilised; such occurrences naturally made the cars unpopular with their passengers, who were sometimes obliged to finish journeys on foot. Perhaps the only thing that could be said for the Clayton cars, apart from the bright touch of colour which they brought to the proceedings with their handsome livery of green and cream, was the fact that they provided the passenger with a much higher standard of comfort.

It was now the turn of the Sentinel railcars, which had in the meantime been building up a somewhat better reputation than their cousins the Claytons. In September 1930 No 12E, shortly to be renumbered 43307, was transferred to Annesley from the nearby GN shed at Colwick, where it had worked for some time on trains to Pinxton and Derby. This vehicle was one of the original trial cars that had been built for the LNER in 1925 in conjunction with Cammell Laird's, and despite the fact that its chain drive was regarded as antiquated by 1930, it appears to have given satisfaction on the 'Dido', as it stayed at Annesley until withdrawn in 1940.

During this lengthy period it had assistance at various times from its original stablemate of 1925, No 43306, which had short spells at Annesley in 1931 and 1932, and then settled down as regular partner from July 1937. It is likely that the reason for at least the first two visits was that No 43307 was under repair, and perhaps the reason for its arrival in 1937 was to cover for failure on the other car. Prior to this it had been necessary for a normal train to be turned out if No 43307 failed, and this meant that one of Annesley's 'N5s' or 'Pom-poms' was tied up until the car could be got back into traffic.

Drivers particularly associated with the railcars were Messrs Hoe, Fisher and Archer, all of whom had been specially passed to drive the Sentinels, as ordinary drivers were not allowed to handle them. Considerable skill had to be exercised both by driver and fireman if good results were to be obtained from these temperamental machines. Best coal was always supplied, usually from Rother Vale, Manvers, or Denaby, and this had to be specially prepared at the shed, being broken up into small pieces and manhandled in sacks into the vehicle, as the Sentinels did not have the handy exterior bunker of their predecessors the Claytons; later however they were modified with the addition of a hatchway in the roof, which greatly eased the work. Firing the Sentinels was a novel activity for a man used to a 'Tiny' or 'Four-cylinder'; using a small implement resembling a domestic fireside shovel, he scooped coal through an opening in the top of the vertical boiler, and although this task could not be described as very arduous, the heat of the completely enclosed compartment made the work uncomfortable.

The railcars were serviced at Annesley Loco, and the work was done between late morning and early afternoon during a spell between trips. However, as the vehicles were classed as coaching stock, rather than being the property of the Loco Running Department, all cleaning was done at the carriage sidings at New Basford, and the car was scheduled to arrive there at 3.50pm daily, leaving for Bulwell Common at 5.6pm. By the mid-thirties the inevitable economy measures had drastically altered this arrangement, and the visit to New Basford was restricted to Monday only. The task of cleaning out the car after a week of continuous use is not likely to have been a popular one among the New Basford staff. The new cleaning rota also meant that the once-smart cream and green bodywork deteriorated somewhat.

The notably poor quality Annesley water was as unkind to the railcars as it was to conventional loco-motives, and so it was arranged that as far as possible replenishment should take place at Bulwell Common; thus the 'Dido' was often to be seen standing by the Bulwell water-column.

At some date in the mid-1930s a further refinement was introduced into the service with the provision of a stop at Hollinwell and Annesley station, which was directly adjacent to the yard and thus convenient for the shunters and other staff. The enginemen benefited from yet another improvement when Annesley South Junction Halt was opened shortly afterwards. Intended purely for the railwaymen, this was a characteristically spartan structure with 'station buildings' consisting of a humble shelter on the up platform, but it was highly convenient for the Loco. Only on certain specified trips did the 'Dido' call at the new halt, or at Hollinwell and Annesley, these calls depending on which staff were using the train at a particular time.

Despite the short trips, the 'Dido' working was heavier than appeared on the surface, since it operated right round the clock. Over the full seven-day cycle the aggregate mileage was about 250, and taking the gradients into consideration this was no easy task for a lightweight machine such as a railcar. In all probability this is the story behind the early disappearance of the Clayton cars, and the fact that the Sentinel-Cammells lasted so long speaks extremely well for them. By the end of the 1930s however the latter were all but life-expired, and after a period during which later cars of the same or similar types were used, the 'Dido' entered yet another interesting stage of development with the introduction of push-and-pull working. As this took place during the war however, the story must be told another time.

132
Annesley Loco on a Saturday afternoon in July 1937, a bird's-eye view from the top of the coaling plant. From left to right in the foreground are the turntable, hand coaling-stage and water treatment plant. Almost out of use by this time, the coaling-stage was unique on the GC London line in having a gable roof instead of the usual water tank; no doubt this was because of the bad quality of Annesley water. Next to the loco coal wagons are redundant locomotive tenders used as sludge carriers for the water treatment plant. The enginemen's barracks may be seen directly against the GN line, and behind the shed building is the tree-lined drive to Newstead Abbey. *W. Potter*

133
Colwick engines visited Annesley quite frequently, and here 'K2' No 4646 is seen at the side of the shed building in 1929. *G. Coltas*

134
The 'Dido' in GCR days. Sacre 4-4-0 No 444B at Bulwell Common in 1920. *F. H. Gillford/Authors' Collection*

135
One of the diminutive Sacre 2-4-0 tanks, No 449B at Neasden Loco. This engine worked the Annesley 'Dido' for a short time. *Authors' Collection*

136
'D12' No 439 is still in GCR livery on Annesley shed on 21 July 1923. It worked the 'Dido' regularly at this time. *W. Potter*

136

137

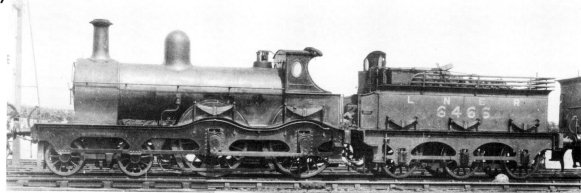

138

137
A 'D12' in LNER livery this time. No 6466, seen at Annesley on 6 June 1926, was withdrawn later in the year.
W. Potter

138
In full GC livery on 21 July 1923, Annesley's 'D9' No 1022 shows off the handsome lines of a Robinson passenger engine. It is pictured at its home shed. *W. Potter*

139
The proud 'D9s' were sometimes employed on the 'Dido'. Here is No 6016 with the unmistakable workmen's coaches at Annesley Loco on 6 June 1926. *W. Potter*

139

140
Clayton Railcar No 2122 *Railway* was in north Lincolnshire before moving to Annesley. It is seen here at Grimsby Town station in the spring of 1929, with fireman Bill Botham in the picture. *Authors' Collection*

141
Sentinel No 43307 at Annesley in July 1937. This was the occasion of a visit by a party of enthusiasts from Manchester, who inspected the shed at the invitation of the Foreman Mr Rickards, seen leaning from the window smoking a pipe. *W. Potter*

140

141

142

142
'J10' engines sometimes deputised for failed railcars on the 'Dido'. Here is No 849 at Annesley Loco on 21 July 1923. *W. Potter*

143
'Q4' No 1177 is a visitor from Mexborough. Annesley shed, 21 July 1923. *W. Potter*

144
Annesley sidings, 1929, 'C14' No 6124 has arrived with the 'Dido' and is about to run round the train. The carriage has

blacked-out windows and one of the doors is marked 'private', probably to prevent members of the public from entering. *G. Coltas*

145
'O4' No 6214 was an Annesley stalwart, based there throughout the period between the wars. It was pictured on its home shed in July 1939. *W. Potter*

146
A 'Humpy'. No 421 was working an Annesley Carriage and Wagon shops pilot when photographed on 21 July 1923. *W. Potter*

143

144

145

146

147

147
A fitting note to conclude on. 'D12' No 6464, a survivor from Victoria's time, is on the Carriage and Wagon Dept's train at Bulwell Common in July 1926.
T. G. Hepburn/Rail Archive Stephenson

148
An example of one of the specially built workmens coaches employed on the 'Dido'. The last example was condemned in November 1934.

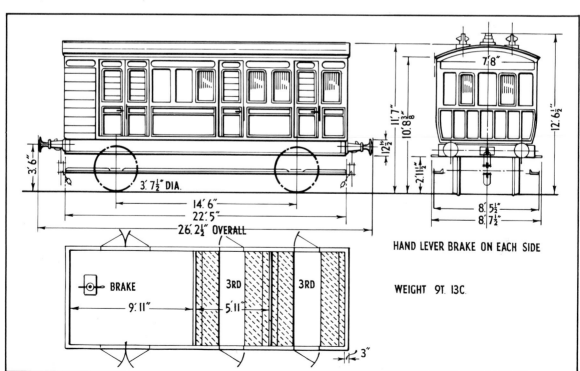

HAND LEVER BRAKE ON EACH SIDE

WEIGHT 9T. 13C.

148

Index